A Beginning Guide to Alternative Assets – There's hills in them thar gold!

A Textbook for Alternative Assets

By Howard Lodge, PhD and Joseph F. Rinaldi, III

This book is intended to show how assets other than stocks, bonds and "cash" are created and valued. It combines funded (you pay money at the beginning) and unfunded (you pay little money at the beginning –"derivative") assets into one conceptual framework.

A Beginning Guide to Alternative Assets There's hills in them thar gold!

A Textbook for Alternative Assets

Published by CreateSpace

Nonfiction/Textbook/Alternative Assets/Derivatives

First Edition (May, 2014)

ISBN:1495419665

EAN-13: 9781495419669

Acknowledgements: The Authors would like to thank Pavan Rangachar for his many suggestions on improving the book.

Introduction - Why another book on Alternative Assets?

Section I. Overview of Traditional & Alternative Assets.

Section II. The Value Drivers of Alternatives - basic level.

Section III. Numbers, Bloody Numbers.

Section IV. Alternative Value Drivers (Advanced Level).

Introduction - Why another book on Alternative Assets?

The authors have taught derivatives and alternative assets to Wall Street finance professionals, MBA's at top business schools and "buy-side" portfolio managers. What they believe is lacking is a book that builds on concepts and is a general book. Too often, the approach of "unscrew head, pour in sand (a bunch of details), screw head back on" is the norm.

This book attempts a middle ground. The desire is to present enough detail to meaningfully get an answer to a question but not so much that the forest is lost in the trees. Thus, it is viewed better to tell the reader the overall concepts and then focus in rather than just jumping into the deep end. The important concepts will be presented in ways that will hopefully stimulate the reader to look at them in his or her own way.

There are three parts to this work – the Book itself presenting the concepts, Appendices to show concepts in numerical detail and Exercises to allow essay answers to the concepts.

The authors believe in the "spiral" approach to learning: present the overview and then go through the material again in more detail. This allows a complete treatment at each level of detail.

The first level is the first eight Chapters. This could be the core of a VERY brief overview. The rest of the book presents the second level. These two levels could be the basis of an undergraduate course. Finally, the intention is that including the appendices and exercises would allow the book to function at the MBA level.

Chapter 1 presents an overview of traditional assets – stocks, bonds and cash. It covers who creates them, who buys them and how investors are trying to manage them.

Chapter 2 presents an overview of non-traditional or alternative assets. Two matrices are presented to organize all alternatives – funded and unfunded. Derivatives are in the unfunded matrix.

Chapter 3 discusses concepts associated with two of the main columns of the unfunded matrix - forwards and options on forwards.

Chapter 4 continues the focus on the unfunded matrix. It outlines the difference between Exchange and over the Counter (OTC) and gives some history of both.

Chapter 5 begins a discussion of the "Value Drivers" rows in the matrices. It outlines how Fixed Income Rate Derivatives grew out of Securities lending, Repo and Reverse Repo transactions.

Chapter 6 discusses the next value driver in alternatives – Credit.

Chapter 7 presents the rest of the value drivers – Equity, Commodity, Currency and Real Estate.

Chapter 8 discusses structured paper. Securities are put in a trust and the cash flows are directed to "tranches" that investors buy.

Chapter 9 gives some numerical background allowing us to go forward at a deeper level.

Chapter 10 contains some details on Black-Scholes Option Pricing.

Chapter 11 is a more detailed view of interest rate alternative assets (expands Chapter 5 concepts).

Chapter 12 treats credit alternatives with a deeper view (expands Chapter 6 concepts).

Chapter 13 goes into the other alternatives at a deeper level (expands Chapter 7 concepts).

Chapter 14 goes deeper into structured assets (expands Chapter 8 concepts).

Chapter 15 shows some management techniques that have been used in alternative portfolios- Efficient Frontiers and Monte Carlo Simulation.

Chapter 16 presents current legal and regulatory issues in alternatives.

Chapter 17 presents accounting and tax issues.

Chapter 18 shows some case studies.

Chapter 19 suggests ways alternative programs can be set up in different businesses – retail brokerage, institutional, etc.

Chapter 1. An Overview of Traditional Assets – Stocks, Bonds, Cash.

1A. Who issues (creates) traditional assets?

All assets are initially issued by some legal entity and are meant to get money today for promise of future returns that are attractive to the buyer. The assets are in the form of public, 144A and private.

Public issuance means they are securities subject to SEC regulation. Two examples are stocks and corporate bonds. Private issuance occurs in stocks but mainly it occurs in notes and bonds. The issuer does not advertise the issuance to everyone, but only a select few (that must be accredited investors or institutional clients). Securities that are 144A are private securities that may be registered in the future and become public.

The primary market is the market created at issuance. The secondary market is securities traded after issuance. Thus, a trade is secondary if the original buyer sells the security to someone else.

A secondary market in stocks exists as long as the company is functional. In bonds, a secondary market exists until the note or bond matures or default occurs.

1B. What are the classes of traditional assets?

1B1. Stocks

In a public company, stocks represent company ownership. One typically buys the stock on an exchange and a book entry is created in a brokerage account. The stock is registered in "street" name. The broker is the legal owner. Rarely is a physical certificate created and sent to you as in the past.

Since the stock is in your account, you receive all cash flows. Dividends are paid quarterly, but are an uncertain amount. They depend on the company earnings and are a decision of company management. You are mainly looking to make money on price appreciation.

To buy the stock, you pay price only. All future (uncertain) dividends are valued in the price.

Most stock pricing models arrive at price by discounting some future flow from the company. This flow could be earnings, free cash flow, etc. In this regard, stocks are priced similarly to bonds. The question becomes: "what is the appropriate discount rate"? Logically, it should be a rate reflecting the risk of the stock itself. What spread to treasuries is that risky rate?

An example of an alternative pricing approach is comparing stock price divided by the company earnings (the P/E ratio). The measure of earnings is usually before debt interest, taxes, depreciation and amortization are subtracted (EBITDA). A high ratio means the stock in question is expensive relative to other "similar" stocks.

1B2. Notes and Bonds

Notes and Bonds are debt obligations of some company with coupons (interest) and principal ("par"). Typically, notes are maturities from one year to 15 years and bonds mature beyond that. Bills are one year and under.

An example would be a 5 year note. Suppose the price for the note was $100 and the coupon was 5% per year. This is a "par" note – the price of the note is $100 and in 5 years you get your principal/par back of $100 assuming no default. You would get 9 semi-annual coupons of approximately $2.50 per $100 par. The last payment would be the tenth $2.50 coupon + $100 (the coupon plus the principal or "par" amount).

Some semi-annual notes actually pay coupons that may not be exactly $2.50. This is because of the calendar days in a six month period not being equal. Remember, there are 365 days in a non-leap year. Some notes pay exactly $2.50. This is because they assume 30 days per month. Thus, the exact coupon payment depends on the "day count" convention.

A note that is not a par note might cost $80 (or $120). The return now would not just come from the coupons but from the fact that you get par in 5 years ($100), but that is not what you paid for it in the beginning.

One pays price plus accrued interest to buy notes or bonds. The seller gets the coupon interest from the last coupon payment to the day the trade settles or "clears". Call this time period (1 to 2). The buyer will get the full next coupon (1 to 3) but is only entitled to that piece from settlement (2 to 3). Thus, the seller is paid their due interest (1 to 2) on the day of settlement. Although the buyer gets the full next coupon, they only net (2 to 3) since they paid (1 to 2) on settlement.

The clever reader may wonder if the seller is getting the better deal. They get the fractional coupon early from the buyer. The buyer has to wait to get the coupon on the next half year cycle. The answer is that any timing effects are in the price. That is, the worth of the note (price plus accrued) is the present value of all cash flows. If the present value of the accrued interest is too high because it is paid early, the price of the bond will be less because the sum of the two is what is paid and that is what the future cash flow stream is worth.

1B3. Cash or Bills

Bills may or may not have coupons. Treasury bills usually trade at a discount to par with no coupon. Bills are considered "cash" since the maturity is so short.

1C. Who buys these traditional assets?

1C1. Individuals

Individuals typically have these assets in broker accounts. They try to decide what category (stocks, bonds or cash) to overweight and then pick individual examples of the category. The goal of most individuals is to maximize pretax total return. That is, make the account bigger regardless of whether the money comes from interest (coupon or dividends) or price appreciation (increase in stock or bond price). The individual typically worries about taxation of these different sources of money later.

1C2. Mutual funds

Pooling many individuals' assets *should* allow for efficiency since the pooling might allow investments the individual could not make by themselves.

One reason for the word *should* being emphasized is that trading costs are spread out over the investors in the mutual fund. The mutual fund investors go in and out of the fund at one number - the net asset value or NAV. The fund manager goes in and out of the underlying securities paying bid-offer spreads. Thus, one investor trading in and out frequently generates costs another investor must absorb if they are "buy and hold". Ask about active trading penalties before you invest! Avoid funds with securities that have big bid-offer spreads!

Mutual funds are one step up from individual investing in complexity. Mutual funds emphasize pretax total return. Aside from the traditional mutual fund varieties, exchange traded funds exist that minimize expenses. An example is "spiders". They allow one to trade the S&P 500 without buying the individual stocks. One can simply buy a stock that is backed by the 500 individual stocks in a trust.

1C3. Corporations

In corporations, (1) operating units sell a product or service and that allows an asset purchase. Money from the asset purchase offsets the liability. The company earns the spread. The accumulation of the spread over time hopefully creates a (2) surplus. A (3) holding company is formed since the growing business needs management. Employees usually get (4) a pension that is managed with money segregated from the company operating money to protect the retirement of the employees. The method of investment in corporations depends on the source of the funds. That is, these four "pots" of money usually have different investment "goals". For example, the (1) operating units usually buy bonds and hold them. This is because they want a constant asset return. They usually don't want the fluctuation stocks would add. Pension investing (4) usually mixes stocks and bonds since they want to maximize long term return and can afford the stock fluctuation since it is assumed to balance out over time.

1C3a. Operating unit investment

It is interesting to note that corporate America typically invests in bond assets in their operating units. Among the many reasons is that they want a steady and defined stream of cash against the liability so that they can price their product. Stocks don't drive corporate America as they do for individuals or mutual funds.

In addition, corporations think after tax. Since one simple way to reduce taxes is to defer them, they trade as little as necessary. Since taxes are assessed at sale, "Corporate America" does not "whip and drive" their trading. It is not due to being lazy but really due to tax deferral!

Another reason bonds are used in operating units is that corporations are forced to reserve against risks in their business. The return the operating unit earns (asset minus liability spread) divided by amount reserved is one measure of a successful investment. It is called return on equity (ROE). Bonds require much less reserves than stocks so using bonds as the asset produces a much higher ROE than the same spread produced by stocks (as the asset).

1C3b. Surplus

Surplus is theoretically the cash "kitty" to protect against the unforeseen. In reality, it typically is a blend of stocks, bonds and cash. The stocks are in there because the investment horizon is unknown. That is, since bonds and cash have fixed maturities and stocks don't, the mixture allows to hopefully earn the higher stock returns and surprises are taken care of with the bonds and cash.

1C3c. Pension

Similar to surplus, Pension liabilities are covered by a mixture of stocks, bonds and cash. However, this is slightly different from surplus because special tax rules and investment guidelines apply that make this a more specialized form of investing.

1C3d. Holding company investment

Usually, few assets are owned at this legal entity. Those that are usually occur because this unit can function as a shock absorber. That is, it is the "emergency" ward in the company. If an operating company has a bad asset, the holding company can backstop the operating company with an additional investment to support the liability. This way, the company products are less subject to changes in simply the investment side of the business.

1D. How do people manage traditional assets?

The matrix of technical and fundamental, top down and bottom up, captures many styles. Technical and fundamental data allow us to pick top down (sectors) or bottom up (individual stocks). These sector or stock choices are refined by many additional techniques. Choices might ultimately have associated risk and return judgments.

1D1. The Style Matrix

Technical means the manager looks at past data and tries to deduce a trend that will occur in the future. For example, some stock has hit a top in price over the last three days. It is "capped" there unless it "penetrates" the top and then it is in "breakout".

Fundamental means the manager looks at the financials of the company to determine worth. This usually means they try to deduce future cash flow (usually from earnings) and see if it is greater than other similar companies.

Top down means one tries to pick stock categories rather than individual stocks. Will the consumer goods sector perform better than the financial sector, etc.?

Bottom up means the opposite. One concentrates on individual stock factors and might buy a "good" stock in a mediocre "sector".

1D2. Risk and return

Do you want 5% almost every month or something that averages 6% but some months is 0% and some 12%? Return and risk are constantly being traded off.

The tradeoff typically depends on the cushion one has. If you can afford to take more risk, you typically will take more except for other factors (such as being close to retirement).

More about this later. Suffice it to say that most financial approaches lead to risk / return judgments and they are summarized systematically.

Chapter 2. An Overview of Alternative Assets.

There is a continuum of non-traditional assets ranging from more to less traditional. They can be funded or unfunded. This means you must have your own money to invest (a funded investment) or not (an unfunded investment). If you invest money in a fund of these, your investment is funded but the fund manager may do some of the investments in derivative form, thus leveraging your funded investment by the unfunded derivative.

The Appendix presents the two Alternative Matrices – funded and unfunded.

2A. The Funded Matrix

The funded matrix is further divided into unstructured and structured (columns) and Value Drivers (rows). The Value Driver is the major factor driving price.

2A1. Funded and Unstructured

2A1a. Hedge Funds

Hedge funds exist across all value drivers. The commonality is that they try to hedge-get the best return with controlled risk. Also, most hedge funds invest in tradable assets, not private ones that don't trade. Hedge fund investors "do a trade"; private equity investors "do a deal".

More completely, even primarily equity hedge funds differ from private equity in that (1) they are hedged, (2) they are liquid and marked to market, (3) they typically don't try for control (manage the company), (4) they are typically LLC's and not partnerships. In an LLC, any liability the company generates does not flow through to the individuals who formed the company. It flows through to the company. In a partnership, there are limited partners (LP's) and general partners (GP's). The "shock absorber" in a partnership is supposedly the GP's. They "cushion" the LP's investment.

There are several classic strategies in hedge funds (with both equity and other value drivers).

Equity Long / Short

This is the earliest hedge fund strategy. You buy a cheap stock and sell short a rich one. Selling short means you sell something you don't own. You borrow the stock, sell it immediately and then buy it back in the future. If the future price is below the original price, you make money. So, you want the long stock to go up and the short one to go up less (or maybe even go down!).A second way this strategy makes money is to be net long as the market moves up and net short as the market moves down. That is, getting market direction right and not being neutral to market movement because one is net long or net short.

Equity Market Neutral

Clearly, like Equity Long/Short, but the strategy tries to be indifferent to general market movement. You make money only by correctly picking rich stocks to short and cheap stocks to buy.

Convertible Arbitrage

This strategy is popular in countries that don't have developed traditional equity or debt markets. An issuer issues a bond with an equity "sweetener". That is, the issuance is like a bond (has a coupon and final principal) but allows you to convert to equity if stock prices go up. You typically can buy converts cheaply and hedge the equity and bond components and pick up yield. Thus the trade has three parts – own convertible bond, apply bond credit and interest rate hedge and equity upside (call) hedge.

Fixed Income Arbitrage

This strategy is similar to equity long / short but in bonds. You might find two bonds equally valued but one is cheaper to borrow than another. You borrow and buy the cheaper one and short the more expensive one.

Short

The manager is always "short the market". This can be in equities, bonds, currency, etc. Trading from the short side of the market is very different than the long side. Adding to the above information on shorting, in this trade you borrow the security and sell it today. During the trade, you pay the coupons (bonds) or dividends (stocks) to the person you borrowed from. They (or the broker who arranged the trade) keep the cash from the trade as security for you replacing the security at the end of the trade. They pay you interest on this cash. Thus, there is a net flow – you get interest on the cash and you pay the coupon/dividend.

Finally, you unwind the trade by buying the security from someone else with the cash and the trade ends. You make money if the price you buy it back is lower than the initial sold price.

The risk is you may not be able to get the security to unwind the trade. It may be a small issue, an issue in demand, etc. Thus, this is a very technical trade. You don't own the security and it may be difficult to buy back to cover the short when you want to. Thus, you must short securities you can get back! If not, be prepared to watch the price of the security move in the market and you can't do anything about it! You are in a "short squeeze".

Emerging Markets

These strategies usually are currency or bond strategies. You are typically long and rarely are these strategies hedged. One is simply long emerging market country securities hoping they will prosper.

Event

One can trade financial events. These events can range from anticipating corporate takeovers to trading after an event has happened. An example of anticipating corporate takeovers would be to buy the stock of the company you think will benefit. Since companies typically overpay for acquisitions (giving birth to the "good will asset"), one buys the company being acquired and shorts the company doing the acquiring.

Buying stressed ($40 per $100 par) or distressed ($20 per $100 par) debt is an example of a trade after a company goes through an event. In this case, the event is that the company credit has been downgraded but one thinks the company will be stronger in the future.

A perfect example of this is buying debt obligations of Ford and GMAC during the financial crisis. Both issues traded at an extreme discount to par and offered an investor exceptional total returns.

Macro

In the 1990's, Macro was a major hedge fund approach. Sell short a currency in size and make money because you sell short so much of it. Create value by driving the market.

The strategy can be either systematic or not. Systematic macro strategies use computers to make investment decisions. Non-systematic approaches use other strategies such as fundamental economic views to make decisions. Securities used in a trade are typically government bonds, stocks, currency etc. In summary, economic opinions about countries generate trades in currency or government securities of the countries and the trade is done in size.

Managed Futures

These are technical trades generated by computers that attempt to take out momentary anomalies in stocks, bonds and other liquid futures. There are a great number of trades each day and each trade is done in a very short period of time – the trade is both spotted by the computer and executed by computer. It typically lasts for a short period of time.

Multi-Strategy

Here one combines some of the above strategies for a more diversified fund. It differs from fund of fund strategies in that the different strategies are done by the same manager. In fund of funds, a manager picks fund managers that do the different strategies.

2A1b. Private Equity

A second example of unstructured funded alternatives is private equity. Here there is a main value driver – equity. There are generally two businesses here – LBO and venture.

Leveraged buyout (LBO)

This is the land of suspenders with dollar signs!

The classic private equity deal starts by observing a (say) private company you think will do better except for some problem you think you can fix. That problem is usually management. You think either you or someone else can do a better job.

You get a controlling interest in the company by either buying lots of stock or bonds the company has issued. You get the money to do this by borrowing (hence the leverage part). You get voting (or not) membership on the board and you become an active board member. You make the change and take the company public in an initial public offering (IPO).

You make money two ways. **First**, if the company makes (say) 10% profit but it only costs 5% to borrow the money to buy the company, you make money on the spread until you sell the company. That is called making "carry". **Second,** you sell the company (public or private) for more than you borrowed to buy it.

The net result is the company has more debt in an LBO but it is a better company.

Venture capital

This is the land of dungarees and Silicon Valley.

Venture is providing capital for a new idea. An inventor has a new idea and needs capital to develop the idea. The problem is there are few new good ideas!

Recently a large percentage of capital earmarked for Venture has been directed to the Biotech and Internet areas.

2A1c. Mezzanine Funds

A common debt structure to alternative projects is senior, mezzanine, equity. Different people lend money taking different risks.

The senior debt lender is typically a bank. They take the least risk. If default occurs, they are the first to get "recovery" money.

The mezzanine lender is next. They give money and get either subordinated debt or preferred equity in the project. In a bankruptcy, subordinated debt gets their money after the senior lender but before equity. Preferred equity has a coupon (like a bond) but has some equity feature (like some upside). Mezzanine securities are put in a fund and investors can buy into the fund.

The equity lender is last. They usually get common stock but sometimes debt again with "features". They are equity since their securities are gone first in a bankruptcy, not because they must necessarily own stock.

2A1d. Infrastructure Funds

These are funds that make money because of the money spent in energy transportation such as pipelines, rails, highways, etc. For example, they might get a piece of tolls charged on a highway.

2A2. Funded and Structured

There are two steps in creating a funded structured alternative asset. First, the issuer buys assets and puts them in a pool. Second, they create rules that direct the cash flows of that pool to notes investors can buy. These notes are the structured alternative assets as far as an investor is concerned.

The entire structure is put in a trust. The pool is the assets of the trust. The notes are the liabilities of the trust. An investor buys the notes thus repaying the issuer who had to buy the original assets to put in the pool.

There can be one note or a series of notes. If there is a series of notes, they are called tranches (which is French for slice). The pool cash flows are sliced by the rules defining how cash is paid from the pool to the notes.

An example that has only **one note** is a Brady bond. In the 80's, many US banks had made loans to Latin America that appeared might default. The Brady structure (named after Nicholas Brady, Treasurer of the US at that time) mixed these loans with US treasury zeros and issued the mixture as a single note/bond. For example, suppose a ten year zero costs $60 per $100 par, one could spend $40 and buy some loans. If you paid $100 for this mixture, you might get your interest (due to the loans performing) but you should get your principal ($100) back when the US treasury zero matured in 10 years.

An example of a **multiple note** issuance is a commercial mortgage backed security (CMBS). A developer of a shopping mall is lent money and the developer plans to pay the loan back by building a shopping mall, leasing the space and using some part of the lease payments to pay off the loan.

These loans are put in a trust. This is simply an account of a legal entity that promises how it will pay due to a trust indenture. The principal and interest of the loans in the trust are paid to investors in the trust. The investors buy tranches (or slices) of the cash flow of the pool. These are usually notes with coupons and principal payments.

A typical CMBS trust indenture has separate rules for the principal and interest cash flows. The "top" tranche has some fixed principal (say) 70% of the pool's principal. It gets repaid before the "lower" tranches – "mezzanine" and "equity" notes. All notes get their share of interest. Defaults of mortgages reduce the pool and the lowest tranche par. Prepayments reduce the par of the highest tranche. This is an example of a typical "waterfall" set of payment rules.

Other assets structured like this include CMO's (Collateralized Mortgage Obligations-the residential parallel to CMBS), CDO's (Collateralized Debt Obligations – using corporate bonds or credit derivatives), CLO's (Collateralized Loan Obligations), etc.

It is important to note these structures are sold discussing the averages in the pool. Many of the pools were "bar-belled". Many bad loans mixed with good ones. The averages look fine but you face the worst. Don't be fooled!

2B. Unfunded

Derivatives are alternative assets but are treated separately because they are transactions that cost no money today (**are unfunded**), **derive** their value from some other asset and set a price today **requiring** you to deliver the asset in the future (or **a forward**) or giving you the **option** to deliver at a price set today (**an option**).

Derivatives are possible on any underlying asset. The major ones are Interest rates, Credit, Equity prices, Commodity (soft – wheat, hard - gold) and Currency.

Thus, it might be useful to think of derivatives as having the same value drivers as funded but having additional columns – OTC forward and options and Exchange futures and options. In addition, some of the assets in those cells can be structured assets as well as the usual non-structured assets.

It should be noted that forwards and futures usually reference a time period that starts today and ends in the future. However, some forwards and futures are deferred – they reference a time that starts in the future and ends at some further time in the future.

An example of an OTC deferred forward is a swap that starts in 2 years and ends in 3 years. An example of an Exchange deferred future is a 3 month Eurodollar future that starts in 1 year and ends in 1 year 3 months from today.

Note that the concept of deferment is different than observing that there are (say) March, June, September and December futures all offered "today". These futures all start today and end at different times in the future which is different than futures that START at different times than today.

See the Appendix and the Summary below.

2C. Summary of Chapter 2

Much is made of alternative assets being not correlated to traditional assets. Usually this argument is flawed because the comparison is to a single traditional asset (say, stocks) and a hedge fund (which has stocks, bonds, hedges, etc. in it). A better comparison to a hedge fund is a balanced fund or cash! The hedge fund is supposed to be hedged!

Thus, it is tempting to group alternative assets into traditional buckets since there are definitely similarities.

Traditional (public) equity is clearly a candidate to be compared to **private equity**. Private equity should beat public equity because it is less liquid and one has increased the leverage of the company (you borrowed and bought the company). Private equity also has tax advantages to public equity - more about that later.

Traditional bonds might be compared to **structured notes**. Structured notes should beat more traditional bonds because they are less liquid and they have severity risk.

Severity risk occurs since you buy tranches and can be wiped out quickly if you are wrong in your assumptions. For example, say you buy a tranche that has 10 % below you (you are in a structure with an equity tranche of 10% and you own the tranche above it). The good news is that you can have 10% of the pool default with zero recovery and you will not have lost. However, if your tranche is the next 10% and if 20% of the pool is a loss, you will have lost all your money. The traditional investment in the pool will have only lost 20% of their money.

The traditional cash investment should be compared to **hedge funds**. That is, hedge funds are liquid and theoretically hedged, thus have less risk than the other "outright long" alternatives.

All these securities should be thought of as defined by two matrices – funded and unfunded.

The funded examples require cash at settlement. The rows are the primary value drivers and the columns are whether the security is structured or not.

The unfunded examples are derivatives. Again, the rows are primary value drivers. The columns are OTC forwards and options and Exchange futures and options.

See the Appendix for a summary of these two alternative matrices – Funded and Unfunded.

Chapter 3. Forwards and Options – Detail about the Columns of the Unfunded Security Matrix.

3A. OTC Forwards and Exchange futures.

Forwards are agreements to buy something in the future and pay for it in the future for an agreed price today. Thus, we have a buyer and a seller but instead of buying and selling today, we set a price today and exchange money and securities in the future. Note that since the money is exchanged in the future, the future seller has no money to buy the security today. What is a fair price for each person?

We might be tempted to treat the problem as we treat risk reduction in portfolios of traditional assets. That is, the future seller commits to a price today they think most likely in the future but doesn't buy the asset today (since they have no money). Take risk but diversify the risk by having a portfolio of these forwards at different prices.

This market would be cumbersome. Each trade would take forever and since pricing is based on an expectation, the two people would probably never agree.

What we need is a hedge. This is a way to fix the price of the asset in the future but have that process cost nothing today. One solution is to borrow and buy the asset today. If we do that, we fix our cost today and don't care about what the market does in the future. We borrow money, buy the asset, and earn any interim cash flows from the asset. At maturity, we sell the asset to the buyer and pay back the borrowed principal as well as the interest on the principal.

For example, assume an asset costs $100 today. Assume it is a note with a 5% annual coupon and your annual borrowing costs are 3%. The fair one year forward price is $98 in one year.

To see this, consider the end of one year. The seller delivers the security to the buyer. The buyer gives $98. The seller adds the interim cash payments of $5 for a total of $103. The seller pays back the principal ($100) and interest ($3) and the money is fair. Of course, the seller charged some money for the transaction – the bid / offer spread! That is, they put in some "vig" in the forward so that maybe the forward was $98.10.Thus, $.10 was left over for them.

We see **the seller is whole**. That is, $98 + $5 = $100 + $3 or dollars received = Principal borrowed plus interest paid. Of course, being good finance people, since these cash flows occur at different times, it is really the present value of these cash flows that must be equal.

Is the buyer whole? That depends whether the buyer is a hedger or speculator. A hedger has another side. They may be a manufacturer that will get the asset at $98 in the future (through the forward transaction), does something to it and knows they can sell it at $100 in the future. They are worried the price they would have to pay could go to $105 if they didn't buy forward. Yes, they wished they didn't hedge if the price went down to $90 in the future but they locked in the 2 point profit by hedging regardless ($100 sale, $98 purchase) by taking delivery through the forward market.

If the buyer was a speculator, they simply believe the price will be above $98 in the future. They are "long" the asset and can win (price is above $98 in the future) or lose (below $98).

Pricing this way requires the seller of the forward to deliver and the buyer to accept delivery. If the buyer was allowed to walk away, the seller is at risk. Why?

3B. Options on forwards

If one thought they needed to walk away from the forward, they should have purchased an option. **All options look to forward prices to derive worth.**

Call options allow one to buy an asset at a known price (the option strike) at the option expiration date. The above buyer of the forward paid nothing today but has to pay $98 in the future for the asset. When you buy a call option, you pay a small price at the beginning (the call premium), you might strike the option at $98 (at the money forward) and you have the right to walk away. To walk away, you sell your option and get some money back (the market option price when you sell).

Put options allow one to sell an asset. Thus, call owners cheer when prices go up and put owners cheer when the prices go down.

Although possibly confusing, like options, forwards can be unwound at any time also. The difference between unwinding a forward and an option is that if you buy an option, the most you lose is the initial premium since you get paid when you unwind.

Unwinding a forward requires you to pay a fee and you didn't pay one in the beginning. That is, you know the worst case with an option (you lose the initial premium) but the worst case with a forward unwind is possibly unlimited (you are short and the price just keeps going up!). Basically, you must pay the difference between the market and forward price you locked in. More about this when we get into the details of pricing of forwards and options.

3B1. Basic option positions and payoffs at expiration of the option.

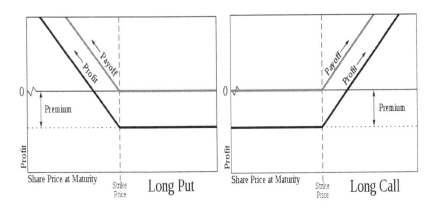

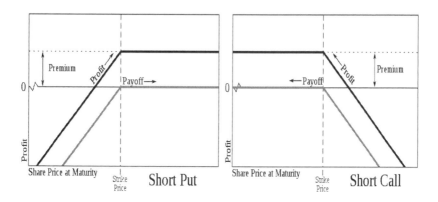

Short Put | Short Call

Buy (Long) a call. You have the option to buy an asset at a fixed price (strike price). You pay a premium (small amount of money) at the beginning. If you don't want to buy, you sell the call on any day if transacted with a broker (they make markets on all securities). The worst case is you sell for nothing. Your worst loss is your call premium.

Sell (Short) a call. You get the call premium in the beginning. **You must make delivery of the asset at the fixed strike price if called.** That is, the option is with the "buy" or long position, not the person who sells the call option. However, this position can be unwound on any day. You may have to pay more than the initial premium to unwind. This could occur if the price of the asset keeps going up.

Buy (Long) a put. You have an option to sell an asset at a fixed price. You pay a premium at the beginning. If you don't want to sell, you can sell the put on any day. Your worst loss is your put premium and that occurs when prices keep rising.

Sell (Short) a put. You get the put premium in the beginning of the trade. You must take delivery of the asset if the long put buyer "puts it (the security) to you". The option is with the long put position. A sold put can be unwound at any day. You may have to pay more than the initial premium to unwind early if the price of the security keeps dropping.

3B2. Option Payoffs prior to Expiration.

The above diagrams show the gain or loss of the four basic option positions **only at expiration**. These values are the "intrinsic value" of the option and are a function of the strike and underlying price of the security.

Prior to expiration, most options (except for deep in the money) have an additional value that adds to the option premium. It is called time value.

An example would be an option with security price and strike the same (at the money or ATM). It has no intrinsic value but with some time left, would have time value and thus a non-zero option premium (option price).

Time value arises because options pay off in a one sided fashion. With time remaining, an option that is ATM can go up or down in price from the current price.

If we have a call and the price goes up, the call is worth more. If the price goes down, there is no change in call worth since the call would expire worthless and it was worthless to begin with. Thus, the more variable the price might be in the future, the greater the time value.

A put has more worth if the price goes down and expires worthless if the price goes up. Thus, like a call it is a "one sided payer" and is also worth more when there is greater expected variability of the security price in the future.

Above we said most options have time value. The options that don't are deep in the money. If an option is deep in the money (security price very different than the strike), the option is like a forward. It is no longer a "one-sided payer". It gains and looses equivalently with up and down security price movement.

Deep in the money options have lost their option properties and might be better exercised (with the resulting security position

~ 23 ~

being established). This is what creates the difference between American and European options (see below).

3B3. Options differ on exercise rights.

European Options can only be exercised at expiration. That is, the buyer of the call can say "Give me the security and I will give you the strike price to buy it" only at expiration. However, since options are bought and sold all day long, European options can be unwound on any day. To do this, one simply pays the market premium (if one initially sold) to buy the option back. If one initially bought the option, one simply receives the market premium (bounded by zero but can be more than the initial premium – the price could soar up!).

American Options can be exercised on any day. This makes them more valuable in certain situations than European Options. For example, suppose you bought a call and the security went way up in price. The option doesn't give coupons or dividends. Since it has the same risk (the option is deep in the money) as the security, American options allow you to exercise and get the coupons or dividends. You are left with a security that has the same risk as the option but gives interim cash flows.

Bermuda options allow periodic exercise, not daily. Thus they are somewhere between American and European and that doesn't mean the Canary Islands! It means Bermuda.

3B4. An example of an exotic option.

Regular options simply compare the strike to the forward price of the security. **Asian options** average something. That something can be the price that is compared to the strike, the strike or both.

The typical Asian option averages the price that is compared to the strike known today. For example, suppose one buys a call option struck at $100 that expires in one year. It might average the end of month prices and compare that average to determine if you are paid.

3C. Summary of Chapter 3

Forward prices assume the person setting the price for future delivery hedges themselves. The simplest hedge is to buy the security today and "carry it". That means, over the life of the transaction (today to forward delivery date), get the coupon/dividend and pay the cost to borrow the money to buy the security today. The spot price and "net carry" define the forward price.

Options are priced by assuming a distribution of future results centered at the forward. If the distribution is symmetric, puts and calls struck at the forward cost the same today. This is formally called "put-call parity".

Chapter 4. Over the Counter Derivatives as compared to Exchange Derivatives – more about the Unfunded Security Matrix Columns.

The picture most people associate with derivative execution is people on an open floor jumping up and down. This is "open outcry" Exchange execution but it is gradually being replaced by electronic execution – all done with computers.

4A. What is an exchange?

An exchange is a marketplace where (1) securities, (2) derivatives, and (3) other financial instruments are bought and sold. Out of these three exchange markets, the stock market (securities) is the most followed but the derivatives market is much bigger than the stock market in terms of size of underlying assets.

A derivatives exchange traded market is a market where individuals' trade standardized contracts that have been defined, structured/created by an exchange. Example of derivatives exchanges are the CME Group (www.cmegroup.com), NYSE Euronext (www.euronext.com), Eurex (www.eurexchange.com), BM&F BOVESPA (www.bmfbovespa.com.br) and The Tokyo International Financial Futures Exchange (www.tfx.com.jp).

The exchange that is developing the contract must determine the underlying asset, quality, contract size, maturity months, delivery arrangements (cash settled and deliverable), deliverable months, price limits, and price quotes.

4B. What does a clearing house do for an exchange?

It manages the exchange. In short, it makes sure trades clear – both sides go away "flat" and happy to/with each other. When the dust settles, the trades are finished and any obligation is over. This is mainly done through margining.

Basically, a clearinghouse acts as an intermediary in futures transactions. It guarantees the performance of the parties to each transaction. The whole purpose of the margining system is to eliminate the risk that a trader who makes a profit will not be paid.

Clearing arrangements vary across industries. However, common elements of clearing houses are that they:

1. Guarantee the traders will honor their obligations (solves trust issues).
2. Make traders obliged to the clearing house, not to other traders.
3. Make each exchange use the clearing house to settle trades.
4. Allow clearing houses to be part of a futures exchange (division, or a separate entity).

4C. How does the clearing house margining system work?

A margin account is opened and allows the investor to borrow or use leverage to transact business. The amount that must be deposited before any transactions occur is called the initial margin. At the end of each trading day, the margin account is readjusted or revalued to reflect the investors gain or loss in that day, i.e., the account is marked-to-market (MTM).

The investor is entitled to withdraw any balance in the margin account that exceeds the initial margin. To ensure that the balance in the margin account never becomes negative, there is a maintenance margin, which is typically lower than the initial margin. If the margin account falls below the maintenance margin, the investor receives a margin call. The investor is required to deposit an amount that makes the margin return to the initial margin requirement. This deposit if referred to as the variation margin.

4D. What is the history of the exchange?

Derivatives exchanges have been in existence for a long time. In 1848, the Chicago Board of Trade (CBOT) was created to bring farmers and merchants together. The main task was to standardize the quantities and qualities of the grains that were traded. A few years later, the first futures-type contract was developed, known as a "*to-arrive contract*". This led to interest from speculators who found that trading the contract was a better alternative to trading the grain itself. In 1919, the Chicago Mercantile Exchange (CME) was established as a rival futures exchange to the CBOT. In the present day, futures exchanges exist all over the world. The CME and CBOT merged to form the CME Group in 2007.

The Chicago Board Options Exchange (CBOE) started trading call options on 16 stocks in 1973. Options had previously traded before 1973, but the CBOE was the first create a structured market with well-defined contracts. Put options started trading on the exchange in 1977. As of today, the CBOE trades options on over 2,500 stocks and many stock indices. Both futures and options are popular contracts to trade among investors. As with futures, options are now traded globally on other exchanges.

4E. Electronic Markets

The advent of electronic trading has eliminated the need for exchanges to be physical places. Many traditional trading floors are closing, and the communication of orders and executions are being done entirely electronically. The Eurex, the world's second-largest futures exchange, is completely electronic. Many others, as they phase out floor trading, offer both floor and electronic trading. The CME Group maintains both the open outcry system and electronic trading. Electronic markets have given rise to algorithmic trading which allows a computer program to automatically trade without the need of a human.

4F. Market size of Exchange Traded products

The Exchange-traded market for derivatives is massive in size. According to an estimate by the Bank for International

Settlements, the exchange-traded outstanding notional was 24 trillion as of December 2012 (www.bis.org/statistics/derstats.htm).

4G. What are OTC Derivatives Markets?

The over-the-counter market is much larger than the exchange market. The unit of size is "notional" and is measured in par (interest rates and credit) or market value (equities and other classes).

Pre Dodd-Frank implementation, trades are done over the phone between two parties. Financial institutions are generally the market makers for the products traded on the OTC market, which means they are always ready to quote a bid price and offer price to a client. They take principal risk – they may not be able to fully hedge their position and may be subject to market movement.

Because of this, each financial institution determines who their clients are and makes them sign legal documents. The most important document defines how trading is done and disputes handled - the ISDA. A part of that document (technically an Annex) is the Credit Support Annex (CSA). The CSA defines how margining is determined. This process is subject to change when Dodd-Frank becomes active.

A major advantage of the OTC market is that there is no specified terms set by an exchange, which allows the parties to make mutually beneficial deals.

A disadvantage is that only two firms are trading. If one goes bankrupt, will the ISDA and CSA hold up in bankruptcy court or will they be thrown out and bankruptcy laws prevail?

4H. History of OTC Derivatives Markets

Since the OTC market does not have a "place" like an exchange, it is very hard to track the history of the market. OTC Derivatives markets are believed to have been around since the times that people would barter goods. It is believed that parties would use a vessel (this represented a contract agreement) and would impress the terms of the commodity size, amount and the transaction date (delivery date) on the vessel.

4I. Market Size of OTC Derivatives Market products

The OTC market is the largest market in the world. According to the Bank for International Settlements, as of December 2012 the OTC notional was $589.4 trillion (www.bis.org/statistics/derstats.htm). We need to keep in mind that the notional value of an Exchange or OTC transaction is not the same as its mark to market. For example, consider the currency OTC trade that promises to buy 100 million US dollars with British Pounds at predetermined exchange rate at 1 year. The notional is $100 million, which is the value used in the $589.4 trillion. However, the mark to market value of the contract might be only $1 million since the market hasn't moved much since the trade was originated. The Bank for International Settlements estimates that the value of all OTC contacts outstanding in December 2012 is about $21.8 trillion on a mark to market basis.

4J. Comparison of Exchange Traded Futures vs. OTC

Forward Markets

The main differences between Forwards and Futures are:

1. Forwards are private contracts, futures are listed on the Exchange, publically observable and standardized.
2. Forwards usually reference one date but futures list multiple dates at one time.
3. Forwards and futures are both marked daily but margin money is typically called for daily only with futures.
5. A CSA defines how forwards are margined. Futures rules are uniform and defined by the Exchange.

Both futures and forwards are agreements to buy or sell an asset at a certain price at a certain future date. Since forward contracts are between two private parties, there is always the risk that one of the parties may not honor the contract. This risk is currently controlled and managed through legal documents – ISDA's and CSA's.

Futures contracts are traded on an exchange and are standardized. A range of delivery dates is typically specified. They are settled daily and normally closed out prior to maturity. Since the parties involved in futures transactions have to use a clearinghouse as an intermediary, it guarantees that there is virtually no credit risk. The only exception is that if margin is not posted, one member must stand in for the other. That is, the exchange system creates a linkage between members that can create a too big to fail situation.

4K. Users of Exchange Traded Markets and OTC Markets.

Hedgers - Hedging involves taking an offsetting position in a derivative in order to balance any gains and losses to the underlying asset. Hedging attempts to eliminate the volatility associated with the price of an asset by taking offsetting positions contrary to what the investor currently has.

Speculators - Speculators make bets or guesses on where they believe the market is headed. For example, if a speculator believes that a stock is overpriced, he or she may short sell the stock and wait for the price of the stock to decline, at which point he or she will buy back the stock and receive a profit. Speculators are vulnerable to both the downside and upside of the market; therefore, speculation can be extremely risky.

Arbitrageurs - A type of investor who attempts to profit from price inefficiencies in the market by making simultaneous trades that offset each other and capturing risk-free profits. An arbitrageur would, for example, seek out price discrepancies between stocks listed on more than one exchange, and buy the undervalued shares on one exchange while short selling the same number of overvalued shares on another exchange, thus capturing risk-free profits as the prices on the two exchanges converge. In short, arbitrageurs make hedging efficient.

4L. Regulation of Exchange Traded & OTC Markets

Futures markets in the US are currently regulated federally by the Commodity Futures Trading Commission (CFTC, www.cftc.gov). The CFTC was established in 1974 and is responsible for licensing futures exchanges and approving contracts. The CFTC also licenses all individuals who offer services to the public and doesn't take disciplinary action but forces the exchanges to disciplinary actions.

The NFA was formed after the CFTC in 1982. The NFA's objective is to prevent fraud and to insure that the market operates in the interest of the public. The NFA monitors trading and can take disciplinary action when appropriate.

The SEC (Securities & Exchange Commission, www.sec.gov), the Federal Reserve Board (www.federalreserve.gov), and the US Department of the Treasury (www.treas.gov) all have claimed jurisdictional rights over some aspects of futures trading (concerning effects on cash instruments).

4M. Types of Exchange Traded Products

The nine top CME derivatives that were traded in each category are listed below, in order, as of August 5th, 2013.

Agriculture - (1) Corn Options, (2) Corn Futures, (3) Soybean Options, (4) Soybean Futures, (5) Wheat Futures, (6) Wheat Options, (7) Soybean Oil Futures, (8) Lean Hog Futures, (9) Live Cattle Futures.

Energy - (1) Natural Gas European Options, (2) Crude Oil Options, (3) Henry Hub Swap Futures, (4) Crude Oil Futures, (5)

PJM Western Hub Real-Time Off-Peak Calendar Month 5 MW Futures, (6) Natural Gas (Henry Hub) Physical Futures, (7) PJM Dayton Hub Real-Time Off-Peak Calendar Month 5 MW- Futures, (8) PJM Northern Illinois Hub Real-Time Off-Peak Calendar Month 5MW Futures, (9) Henry Hub Penultimate NP Futures.

Metals - (1) Gold Options, (2) Gold Futures, (3) Silver Options, (4) Copper Futures, (5) Silver Futures, (6) Platinum Futures, (7) Palladium Futures, (8) Palladium Options, (9) Platinum Options.

Equity Index - (1) E-mini S&P 500 Futures, (2) E-mini S&P 500 Options, (3) E mini NASDAQ 100 Futures, (4) S&P 500 Options, (5) S&P 500 Futures, (6) E mini Dow Futures, (7) E mini S&P Mid Cap 400 Futures, (9) E mini S&P Weekly Options Wk2.

FX (Currency) - (1) Euro FX option (American), (2) Euro FX Futures, (3) Australian Dollar Futures, (4) Japanese Yen Futures, (5) Japanese Yen Options (American), (6) British Pound Futures, (7) Australian Dollar Options (American), (8) Canadian Dollar Futures, (9) British Pound Options (American).

Interest Rates - (1) Eurodollar Futures, (2) Eurodollar Options, (3) Eurodollar 2yr MC Options, (4) Eurodollar 3yr MC Options, (5) Eurodollar 1yr MC Options, (6) 10 yr Note Options, (7) 10yr Note Futures, (8) 5yr Note Futures, (9) 5yr Note Options.

Chapter 5. Evolution of Fixed Income Rate Derivatives.

On to the Value Drivers of the two matrices! This Chapter is about how OTC rate forwards and Exchange Rate Futures grew out of securities lending and the Repo/Reverse markets. Lending and Repo/Reverse trades are alternative assets.

5A. Securities Lending

Most assets in the firm's operating companies are in the form of notes/bonds (see the traditional asset section). There are many reasons for this but two main reasons are stability of earnings and notes/bonds can be easily lent. That is, different than an individual's typical traditional investing strategy (including perhaps 60% equity), operating companies of major firms have little use for equities backing their product. It would be very difficult to plan salaries because of the uncertainty of earnings. Equities move in price too much!

Many securities can be lent but we will stick to notes/bonds since that is mainly what corporate America lends. When corporations lend securities, they receive cash from someone and give that someone "perfected interest" in the security. This means if the firm doesn't give the cash back (typically the trade is done settling next day), the lender of cash can take the security. Thus, securities lending is a form of collateralized borrowing. When you lend a security you are borrowing cash using the bond as assurance you will perform in the future.

The securities lender/cash borrower pays interest on the cash received but can invest the cash in another instrument. If the new investment earns more than the interest paid on the cash, additional earnings can result. Thus, if the firm is an insurance company, we have (1) person buys insurance, (2) the company buys security with cash from selling insurance, (3) the company lends the security out and gets cash, and (4) the company invests cash in a second asset. Thus, two spreads are earned, one between the security and the insurance liability and the second between the security bought from borrowed cash and the rate that is paid to borrow the cash.

This creates leverage in the company since money is borrowed. For every (say) $100 coming from sale of product, the firm now has $200 assets and $200 liabilities.

This trade is unwound by having the one day investment mature. The firm gives the cash from the security bought with borrowed money back to the broker which repays the loan. The broker then gives the original security back to the firm and that security continues to support the original insurance liability.

5B. Repo and Reverse Markets

The "**textbook**" definition of a Repo is typically a trade in which the firm (1) sells a security "today", (2) gets cash "today" for the security sale and (3) agrees to repurchase the security in the future for a price agreed to today. The firm does a Reverse if it (1) buys a security "today", (2) pays cash for it "today" and (3) agrees to sell the security back in the future for a price agreed to "today". The firm earns interest on the cash lent.

In practice, the trader at a good credit institution simply agrees to purchase (Repo) a security in the future for a price agreed today or sell it (Reverse). If these positions move against the trader, collateral is requested. We will discuss these concepts going forward as defining Repo's and Reverses.

A Repo is different than the previously described securities lending trade. In a lending trade, you "post" the security as assurance you will give back the cash borrowed.

In both a Repo and a lending transaction, you are long the market. You make money if prices rise. In a reverse, you make money if prices fall.

Most trades are settled net in the future on the forward part of the Repo/Reverse – cash is delivered, which is the difference between (1) the market and (2) price set through the Repo/Reverse.

For example, a Repo at $100 settles for $1 if the market price at the end of the trade is $101. You gain if prices go up.

A Reverse gains if prices go down. This is because you agree to sell in the future at prices set today. If prices drop in the future, the money you get on the sale is greater than market. You have sold high and can buy back low for a profit.

5C. How the three forward transactions are used

The above three "forward" transactions are with specific securities. **Lending** is one of the primary cash management tools of business. It allows for daily cash management. You lend out your securities and use the cash as you wish. You don't have to invest in a second security. You could repay a debt today and use excess cash tomorrow to repay the original borrowing of cash.

Repo and reverses are useful for hedges. For example, hedging an acquisition could be accomplished using a Repo. You are going to buy a company. You do a Repo today. You buy the company and get the company's cash and liabilities. It will take you awhile to invest the cash asset back into notes/bonds. Your risk is that rates go down and you have trouble supporting the liabilities. The forward you establish in a Repo will pay you if rates go down in the future. It is your hedge.

A **Reverse** is useful if you are a corporate treasurer and have excess cash today but will have a deficit of cash in the future. You will have to issue notes in the future but you are concerned rates will rise. You do a reverse today. If rates rise in the future, your reverse compensates you for the higher rates of your issuance.

But people became worried about these transactions. Since they were on specific securities, couldn't someone "corner the market" and manipulate prices? What if someone walked away from a reverse, prices went down, the "somebody" owed money and didn't pay? These transactions were between big financial institutions but these institutions can still fail. **For these and other reasons, exchange traded futures were born.**

5D. Fixed Income Rate Futures

You can think of repos and reverses as over-the-counter (custom or OTC trades) that are similar to going long or shorting a future on an exchange such as the Chicago Board of Trade (CBOT/CME).

Consider doing a repo. No money changes hands initially (remember, only the "text book definition" requires an initial sale) and one establishes a price in the future that one can buy a security. With futures, again these is no initial money (except for a small amount of initial margin) and one establishes a price in the future that one can buy a security by taking delivery on the future.

The idea behind a future was to simplify and standardize repos and reverses. Instead of a specific security, one shorted (did a reverse – agreed to a future sale price) or went long (did a repo-agreed to a future purchase price) a generic (say) five year.

The generic aspect was accomplished by pricing the future using a basket of securities. The security that was "cheapest to deliver" was the security the future used for pricing - more about this in the detail section on futures.

In summary, repos and reverses are transactions where something is purchased or sold in the future for a price agreed to today. They are done with a broker and are simply another form of a forward transaction. They are priced by assuming the grantor of the forward hedges themselves.

The hedge for a Repo requires shorting a future since the forward in the Repo requires buying. The hedge for a Reverse requires buying (or going long) a future. Finally, futures are done on public exchanges and are typically referencing one security in a basket of securities.

5E. Interest Rate Swaps

Exchange rate derivatives (for example, bond and note futures) grew out of repo and reverse transactions. Repo and reverses are dealer trades useful for overnight hedging and cash management.

Interest rate swaps had a very different origin. They were created initially to change floating rate borrowing to fixed rates or visa-versa. For example, assume you are a company that doesn't have good enough credit to borrow at a fixed rate for 10 years. The lender might let you borrow at a floating rate. That is, the coupon resets every 3 months based on an index, typically the London Interbank Bank Offer Rate (3 month Libor) which supposedly is the rate London banks charge themselves to borrow and lend money for 3 months.

You can fix that floating rate by doing an interest rate swap. The swap has two components – receive floating and pay fixed. The floating rate received on the swap cancels the floating rate paid on the loan. You are left with the fixed rate paid on the swap.

You have used derivatives to create a "synthetic" fixed rate borrowing. The floating rate terms on the swap are identical to the floating rate terms on the borrowing. It is important to notice the credit of the floating borrowing might be different than the credit of the swap. In this example, the company is the credit on the floating rate borrowing (it pays the floating rate).

The credit on the swap is tricky. Suppose fixed rates have gone down. You are paying 5% but the market is pay 4% (to receive 3 month floating Libor) for 10 years. You are higher than the market by 1% a year for 10 years. On $100 "notional" of a swap, that is $1 per year for 10 years or $10, forgetting present valuing.

The swap notional is like the par of a bond. It is the size of the swap. Said differently, the notional of a swap times the rate times the time of the rate (3 months?) defines the dollar amount to pay or get paid.

Although swaps were created to modify borrowing terms, they can also be used as forwards just like repos and reverses. If you want to short a ten year maturity security for 6 months, **pay fixed** on a swap and receive a floating rate with both "legs" of the swap **starting** in 6 months. At the end of 6 months, unwind (also referred to as pairing-off) the swap. If fixed rates have increased 1%, you should be paid the present value of 1% for 10 years. The same result as above-$10 for every $100 notional of the swap, neglecting present value.

In the above example, note the floating leg isn't an issue. It is floating and as long as the swap didn't start, it is at market because the floating coupon wasn't fixed.

Receiving fixed with a forward starting swap is like a security repo. If rates drop at the end of the period, you get paid. If they rise, you pay.

Paying fixed is like reversing in a security. If rates drop, you pay since you are short and when prices go up, a short pays. If rates rise, you get paid.

Since the typical swap costs nothing today, forward starting swaps are a form of forward transactions. They are like futures, repos, reverses. Money flows from conditions changing **after** the position is established.

It should be noted that the Federal Reserve does Repos and Reverses with dealers. When they do that, the trade is looked at from their prospective. That is, their Repo is the dealer's Reverse. In this chapter, we have looked at it from our perspective and have had the freedom to not have the Fed involved!

Chapter 6. Fixed Income Credit Derivatives.

Credit derivatives insure one against default risk. One person pays a premium and if default occurs, gets paid the insured amount. They are buying default protection on a company. The other side of the trade gets paid the premium and must pay the insured amount if default occurs. Typical terms might be $1 premiums per year for 5 years for an insured amount of $100.

6A. The Buyer of Protection pays a Premium and buys Insurance.

Assume you are the buyer of protection and assume the above amounts. You bought protection because you stand to lose if the company defaults. You pay $1 per year until either (1) 5 years is up or (2) you unwind before 5 years or (3) default occurs. In (1), you simply paid for insurance and thankfully the default event didn't occur.

In (2), you no longer need the insurance. Unwinding the trade might cost or you might be paid. It would cost if the current cost of insurance is (say) $0.75 per year. The company improved in credit in this case. If you had a remaining term of 2 years, the cost would be $.50 to unwind (neglecting present value considerations – see next section). That is, what you are paying per year minus market ($1 - $0.75=$0.25 per year for 2 years).

Conversely, you would be paid if the premium went to $2 per year. The payment would be $1 per year for 2 years or $2, again neglecting present value.

We have just seen that a credit derivative can result in gain or loss without default. It is sensitive to the premium you are paying relative to the current market premium. Thus, like a normal corporate bond, changes in credit spread are reflected in price.

Last, if default occurs, the buyer of protection would receive the insured amount or $100 and give the defaulted bond to the seller.

Thus, the seller pays $100 but gets back recovery of the bond. The contract would then terminate.

In practice, the usual settlement is a net cash settlement. The seller of protection pays $100 minus recovery of the bond to the buyer.

6B. The Seller of Protection receives a Premium and sells Insurance.

In this example, the seller of protection gets paid $1 per year. If (1) above occurs, they got paid $1 per year and didn't have to pay the $100 insured amount. The seller can unwind (2) independent of the buyer. That is, markets are made by allowing buying and selling. If there is an imbalance, the broker takes the risk (called principal risk). The broker might have an inventory of bonds and be happy to be net long protection, for example. He is fine with being long protection on one of his bonds in inventory because if the company defaults, the insurance pays.

The seller would pay on unwinding the trade if the premium went to $2 per year. They are only getting $1 and someone assuming that position would want to be compensated the difference. Of course, that is the $2 the Buyer had to pay, neglecting bid/offer of the broker and present value.

Finally, (3) default requires the seller to pay the insured amount of $100 and get the bond. They are thus out $100 minus recovery.

6C. Definitions of Default

Default definitions for a bond security are (1) Declaration of bankruptcy and (2) Failure to pay. Credit derivatives add a third – Restructuring. Restructuring means the terms of a borrowing the company made is changed to the detriment of the lender. In short, the present value of the payments the company makes is less on some obligation.

Restructuring allowed the banks to say to regulators that buying protection on the company allowed the banks to effectively remove a loan to that company from their books. Any loss on that loan was covered and thus no incremental default reserving was required.

Restructuring creates the potential for abuse. A bank could make a loan to a company, buy protection on the company and decide to restructure the loan the bank just made. The restructuring would trigger a default on the credit derivative but not the bond. Thus, the protection buyer would get (say) $100 from the protection seller and give the bond to the seller. The buyer is whole since they paid $100 for the bond in the beginning and got $100 from the seller. The seller may not be whole, it depends on where they can sell the bond.

To date the only protection against this happening is that the market would shut down if that happened!

6D. Credit Derivative Pricing

Detail on pricing credit derivatives comes later. The central concept is one gets in premium what one expects to lose if default occurs. More formally, Probability of surviving * Credit Derivative premium = Probability of not surviving * Loss if default.

This assumes the buyer and seller are rational and each feels the deal is fair. It also assumes your investment horizon is the same as the one period assumed here (or, in general, the horizon is the same as the maturity of the credit derivative-more about that later).

For example, 98.36% * $1 = 1.64% *$60 says for a credit derivative that matures in 1 period, if the probability of survival is 98.36% and the loss if default is $60, the fair premium is $1. The loss is only $60, not $100 since one is assumed to pay the $100, get the defaulted note and get $40 recovery by selling the note. Thus, the loss is the insured amount minus recovery.

Note that if one knows the market premium ($1), and assumes a recovery ($40), one can solve for the probability of survival since there would then be one equation in one unknown. That is, $p*\$1 = (1-p)*\$60$ or $\$61*p = \$60$. So $p = .9836$.

6E. Does the pricing correspond with Default Tables published by the Rating Agencies?

The short answer is no. Credit derivative pricing is driven by the market. Rating Agency Tables are driven by judgment plus market.

For example, someone trading in the market might buy protection not for default reasons but because they believe the spreads will widen on a credit. Since active trading on credit derivatives exists, wider spreads to buy protection than what one locked in earlier means the buyer gets paid by closing out the position with a broker. Default need not happen to get paid (or pay).

Additionally suppose the hypothetical buyer thinks the event will happen in the next three months. This tenor doesn't trade in the market – only the five year maturity is really liquid.

The result? Five year credit derivative spreads start to widen as they buy protection. This is not because of default concerns over a five year span but because someone believes spreads will simply widen in the next three months! The modeling is slightly naïve in assuming the investment horizon of the investor is the same as the maturity of the investment. Said differently, people buy 10 year notes without expecting to keep the notes for 10 years and make or lose money on yield to maturity changes!

Thus, the modeling is really conditional. Credit derivative results might be comparable to agency default Tables (1) if the investment horizon of the credit derivative investor is the same as the maturity of the investment and (2) if the reason for trading is default, not simply spread widening.

Chapter 7. The Rest of the Asset Classes – Equity (Public and Private), Commodity, Currency and Real Estate

7A. Public Equity Alternative Investments

There are many different types of Public Equity Alternative Investments. This section starts with an overview and then describes some of the equity alternatives (the categories sometimes seem endless).

Overview

As with fixed income, equities have forwards, futures and options. The major difference is the dividend of the stock is not as certain as the coupon of a bond. Perhaps that is why forward pricing in equities is for much shorter periods of time than fixed income. There is simply more uncertainty of the forward pricing!

Regardless of the reason, currently equity futures might go out one year at best. Also, different from fixed income, equity forwards typically increase in price going out in time as compared to fixed income. This is strictly a function of forward pricing – if the dividend rate is smaller than the borrowing rate, one demands more money in the forward price to pay for the excess net cost of carry. This is why, all other factors equal, equity calls struck at today's price (spot price) are more expensive than equity puts but the opposite is true of fixed income options.

Said differently, the phrase "in the money" really relates to the forward price for option pricing purposes. If the strike is $100 and the forward is $103, more than half of the distribution is beyond the strike and the call is worth more than if the call is struck at $103 (at the money forward).

Aside from the dividend issue, another difference between fixed income and equities is that the most popular equity option is on an index –the S&P 500 index. There are several possible reasons for this. For example, the popularity of exchange traded funds or ETF's that are S&P 500 based makes S&P put buying attractive.

Insurance companies offer insurance products with the upside of the S&P 500 and buy calls to hedge themselves. Many hedge funds buy index puts to hedge against disaster.

We will now list some of the equity alternative categories.

7A1. Exchange Traded Funds

An Exchange Traded Fund (ETF) is a security that tracks an index, a commodity or a basket of assets like an index fund, but trades like a stock on an exchange. Unlike Mutual Funds, which have similarities to ETFs, ETFs experience price changes throughout the day as they are bought and sold. In addition, the fees on ETFs are usually less compared to the fees of Mutual Funds.

7A2. Exchange Traded Derivatives

7A2a. Equity Single Stock Futures

Single stock futures (SSF) are contracts between two investors where the buyer promises to pay a fixed price for 100 shares of a single stock at a predetermined point in the future and the seller promises to deliver the stock at the specified price on the specified future date. SSF are traded on the One Chicago Exchange or OCX (http://www.onechicago.com/). Going long a single stock future is similar to holding the underlying stock. Some of the differences are you receive no voting rights or dividend when holding the SSF, you can use leverage to purchase a SSF which means you may use less cash upfront but this makes it a riskier investment, taking a short position in a SSF is easier because there is no uptick requirement, and SSF gives investors flexibility and can be used to speculate, hedge, or take advantage of arbitrage opportunities.

7A2b. Equity Index Futures

Index futures are futures contracts on a stock index or financial index. A futures contract on the index is always cash settled.

Index futures are used by many professionals to hedge their portfolio against market moves. For example, let's say a portfolio manager believes that the markets will move to the downside. The portfolio manager can choose to short the S&P 500 Index future as a way to prevent their portfolio from downside risk.

7A2c. Equity Single Stock Options

Exchange options on single stocks are the most commonly traded equity derivative. Options trade on more than 2500 different stocks. The terms of the contract (the expiration date, the strike price, affects that dividends have on the option price, position limits, etc.) are specified by the exchange. Equity options expire on the third Friday of the month. In the United States, stock options are traded on a monthly cycle. Spacing of strike prices of an option is determined by the price of underlying stock. If the stock is priced between $5 and $25 then the spacing is $2.50, if it is priced between $25 and $200 then the spacing is $5, and the spacing is $10 for any stock that is priced above $200. Stock options are usually not changed when a dividend occurs unless the dividend is large. In the case that dividend is large the strike prices will be reduced by the amount of the dividend.

7A2d. Equity Index Futures Options

An Equity Index Futures Options contract gives you the right, but not the obligation, to enter into a futures contract at a certain futures price by a certain date. The advantage of trading Equity Index Futures Options is that it provides you with more liquidity than the options on the individual members.

7A2e. Equity Index Options

Options can also be traded on the indices such as S&P 500 Index (SPX), the S&P 100 Index (OEX), Nasdaq-100 Index (NDX), and the Dow Jones Industrial Index (DJX). Index options contracts are usually European style. An exception is the S&P 100 Index. It is American style. One option contract is equal to 100 times the index. This means that the holder of a call option receives (S-K) * 100 at option expiration while the writer of the call pays that amount and the holder of a put receives (K-S) * 100 while the writer of a put pays that amount. Here K is the strike price and S is the current stock price.

7A3. Over the counter (OTC) Equity Derivatives

Most OTC Equity derivatives are options. Some have become so common they have special titles.

7A3a. Warrants

A warrant is derivative security that gives the holder the right to purchase securities (usually equity) from the issuer at a specific price within a certain period. They typically have maturities greater than 3 to 5 years. Basically, they are long dated call options. Warrants are often included in a new debt issue as a "sweetener" to entice investors. They give equity upside to debt investments. When they are attached to the debt itself (and not separately issued) they form convertible bonds (see below).

7A3b. Employee Stock Options

These are given to employees as reward for their service. **Nonqualified stock options** require you to pay ordinary income tax on the difference, or "spread," between the grant price and the stock's market value when you purchase the shares ("exercise the option"). **Incentive stock options** (also known as "qualified" stock options because they qualify to receive special tax treatment) defer any tax to when you sell the stock. No income tax is due at grant or when you get the shares through exercise of the option. The tax is deferred until you sell the stock you received through exercise of the option.

7A3c. OTC Exotic Equity Options

OTC Exotic options are non-standardized options created by financial "engineers" to fill hedging needs in the market. Financial institutions, fund managers, and corporate treasuries use exotic options for accounting, tax, legal and regulatory reasons. Some of the more commonly known exotic options are Binary, Asian, and Bermudan options. Binary options are options that pay you a fixed pre-determined amount or nothing. An Asian option is an option whose payoff depends on the average price of the underlying asset during the life of the option. A Bermudan option is an option that can be exercised early but on only certain specific dates. A European option is an option that can be exercised on only one date, which is typically the maturity date of the option. An American option is an option that can be exercised any time before the maturity date. Most exchange traded options are American structured options.

7A4. Equity Swaps

Equity swaps are an agreement to exchange the total return (dividends and capital gains) realized on an equity index for either a fixed or a floating rate of interest (a benchmark rate like LIBOR is commonly used). Equity swaps are executed in the OTC markets by large financial firms, banks and investment bankers.

7A5. Convertibles

A convertible security combines debt and equity exposure. It is a bond or preferred stock that gives you the option to convert your holdings into common stock. The price of the convertible is dependent on the underlying common stock price and the convertible feature (i.e. the number shares you can buy over a stated period) is fixed.

7B. Private Equity Alternative Investments

A private equity fund can contain many different types of investments (or deals). Traditionally, LBO's and Venture would be the majority. However, increasingly these funds are opening up themselves to all the other alternative assets. We will first discuss how funds invest in a deal and then how investors invest in a fund.

7B1. How GP's and the fund invest in a deal

When a private equity manager invests in a specific deal to put into a fund, the type of investment can differ. For example, it can be equity or debt, differ in level of seniority (who gets paid first in a bankruptcy), timing of payback, etc. Defining the character of the contribution and how it will be paid back is called defining the "capital structure" of the fund investment.

Assume the fund makes a $15,000,000 investment in a deal that will go into a fund they are managing. The investment has a capital structure of 40% equity and 60% debt. The deal is sold in 7 years. This might be structured as follows:

7B1a. Initial investment in the deal

The 40% equity tranche might be composed of common equity (10%) and equity preference shares (30%).

The **common equity tranche** would thus total $1.5M (10%) and would be the first loss if the investment loses. The GP might contribute $300,000 (2%) and the fund $1,200,000 (8%).

The **preference shares** would total $4,500,000 (30%) at a 10% yield. These are high dividend shares but the dividend is only paid out at the end. That is, the dividend is capitalized. This makes preference shares a cash flow "shock absorber". It allows for variation in cash flow over time since the dividend doesn't have to be paid out until the deal matures. The shares have no capital appreciation other than the dividend being capitalized (so they are really like a zero coupon bond).

Finally, the debt is perhaps amortized (the principal is paid back along with the interest) over 10 years and is a high yield bond. The business associated with the deal may have financed and distributed this part themselves outside the PE fund.

7B1b. Final distribution of a deal

Between initial and final distributions, cash flows have gone to pay down the debt principal and interest and any equity dividends. At the deal termination (7 years), assume the investment is sold for $17 million. What do the different parts of the capital structure get?

Assume the high yield bond has $3.5M left in principal. These debt investors get paid first.

The preference shares are next. They have appreciated to $8.769 million ($4.5M million * 1.10^7).

The remaining money is split between the Fund and GP equity holders in proportion to their initial investment. For further details, see the Appendix associated with this section.

7B2. How investors invest in the fund

We have just seen how the managers of a fund might invest in deals but how does an investor buy into a fund of private equity deals? What do they get if they invest?

As an investor, you would first commit a sum of money to the fund. If enough commitments are obtained, the fund opens and the investment managers (general partners or GP's) start investing in deals (perhaps as above but there are many variations in how they invest). Thus starts the "drawdown" period where the committed capital is requested from the investor by the GP's to invest in deals.

Cumulative capital drawn down is called "paid in capital". It is the total money the GP has invested of your committed capital. The GP management fee is a percentage of this amount.

As time passes, some of the investments mature and return money to the fund. The rest are marked to market. The total of these two results are decreased by distributions to the investor and "carried interest".

The concept of carried interest is simple – the GP should be rewarded for returns above a certain level in addition to the GP management fee. The execution is complex. For example, should the calculation include the mark on the unrealized investments or just the realized (mature) ones? What if the GP does well one year and not the next? Should the reward be "clawed back" after a bad year? Should it be taxed as Capital or Ordinary Income?

In summary, the investor gets realized results of investing in deals after management fees and carried interest is paid to the GP's. We recommend calculating an investor IRR by having the drawn down capital as negative (outflows) when they occur and the realized inflows positive numbers when they occur. That is, the mark to market is not included.

7C. Commodity Alternative Investments

There are hard and soft commodities. An example of hard might be metals and grains an example of soft commodities.

Commodity derivatives have an aspect to them that the "financial" derivatives don't have. Over the pricing period, there is no "coupon". There is only cost. So, the "normal situation" of the forward prices is that they go up as one observes the price of more distant commodity forwards.

They go up to satisfy the standard way to price derivatives – spot price plus net carry. It's just that net carry only has one entry – cost. At one point in time, a one month forward price might be $1500 for gold, a two month forward $1550, etc. If lower in the far month, a commodity trader calls it "backwardation". Note that "backwardation" is the normal state for fixed income. This is because fixed income carry has two entries – coupon and cost and coupon is greater than cost.

Commodities are very technical. Trade flow really sets the price not the assumed "cash and carry" arithmetic assumed for all other derivatives.

7D. Currency Alternative Investments

One agrees to sell (say) $100 USD to get $90 EURO. A spot transaction settles today and a forward transaction settles in the future. The exchange of USD for EURO occurs at the end of the trade. No money is required at the beginning – these are thus unfunded trades and therefore derivatives.

How does one know if the above exchange of currency is fair?

PPP

If world output was determined by manufacturing and all countries created the same goods, we might have a simple way to determine fair. $100 USD buys in the states exactly the same basket of goods in the states as going to Europe, exchanging $100 USD for $90 EURO "spot" and paying 90 EURO for the basket. This approach is "purchasing power parity" or PPP.

As always in pricing, the best theory is defined by the way the biggest player in the market thinks about value! Since 2/3 of GDP is service, not manufacturing, there is an issue with PPP from the get-go.

Interest Rate Differentials

Since flow of money and investing is involved in everything, interest rate differentials suggest another theory of currency pricing. In the simplest form, buying a USD note denominated in USD and earning interest for some period should equal an amount of money at the end that is the same as the foreign investment described below.

The foreign investment has three parts. First, "today" spot convert your USD to the foreign currency. Second, purchase the foreign investment in the foreign currency. Third, "today" forward convert all foreign currency back to USD in the future. The third step is a currency forward. All three steps are done day one.

This foreign investment should give the same USD in the end if the spot currency rate, forward currency rate and foreign interest rate are "fair". The short hand way of thinking about this is that if one country's interest rate is higher than another, the two currency transactions (spot and forward) should take that advantage out. Currency exchange rates should "level out" any interest rate differentials.

Of course, there are many assumptions this theory makes. For example, are the two countries' credits the same? Does the investment require one forward trade or many forward trades if it has periodic coupons over some period of time?

Finally, it should be noted that most currency hedging in practice simply hedges by selling forward (back into the original currency) the original purchase price. That is, market movement (ending price) and uncertainty about interim cash flows of the investment makes for secondary currency risk in most real life currency hedges.

7E. Real Estate

There are several ways investors can invest in real estate.

Clearly, the first is one's home. Next, there are mutual funds. A third alternative is a REIT (Real Estate Investment Trust). These are entities with pools of investors. Because these REITs pay out a large percent of their income to investors (and it is tax deductible), they pay minimal federal tax. This avoids double taxation. One can typically invest in equity or debt of a REIT as one can with most corporations.

If one has more to invest, one can invest in individual residential or commercial properties. This takes one million and up and is typically outside the scope of an individual investment. This is called a real estate "whole loan".

Finally, one can invest in commercial properties through structured investments. Small pieces can be found of CMBS tranches. See the next Chapter on structured investments.

Chapter 8. Structured Paper.

What are the characteristics of structured paper? What are some examples?

8A. Funded Alternatives that are Structured

8A1. The family of C--'s (CMO's, CLO's, CBO's, CMBS)

One of the earliest structured securities was a **CMO** or Collateralized Mortgage Obligation. Individual residential mortgages are pooled in a trust.

As explained in Chapter 2, a trust is simply a legal entity defined by a trust indenture. The indenture defines the assets and liabilities of the trust. Trustees make sure the trust indenture is followed and the cash flows from the pool of assets get correctly to the notes or tranches. Because the investor pays for the tranches, the person who originated the loans in the pool is paid back and not at risk anymore. Rating agencies define the credit of the tranches.

The principal and interest cash flows from the assets are directed in different ways to the liabilities/notes/tranches of the trust.

The tranches might receive the cash from the pools "pro-rata". This means the proportion they get depends on the tranches size or "par".

The more popular distribution is waterfall. First the most senior tranche gets all principal payments from the pool until the senior tranche par is paid, then the next tranche, etc. All tranches get interest cash flows simultaneously. Prepayment shrinks the pool and the active (top) tranche.

In both approaches, default first reduces the pool and the bottom most active tranche (the current "equity" tranche).

A **CLO** is similar but uses bank loans rather than mortgages. Many of these loans come from private equity. The private equity firm takes over a company by borrowing and buying it. This is called a leveraged buyout or **LBO**. The lender (with an investment banker) pools the loans and investors buy the tranches of the structure. Their purchase price for the tranches flows back to the lender and the lender is free to lend again.

Finally, a **CBO** (Collateralized Bond Obligation) uses bonds in the pool and **CMBS** pools commercial whole loans.

8A2. Credit structured paper

In the purest form, a group of credit derivatives that **sold protection on different credits are in the pool.** Since the buyer of protection pays a premium to the seller of protection, the pool has a cash flow.

Thus, pools of credit derivatives create cash flows that can be "tranched". Again, investors buy the tranches, repaying the issuer that bought the credit derivatives from the original seller of protection.

In a less pure form, corporate notes are used in the pool. This is less pure since notes may have different maturities, be discount and/or premium (price above par) etc.

8B. Unfunded Alternatives that are Structured

8B1. Mortgage TBA's

Perhaps the first structured **unfunded** paper was the residential mortgage TBA. This security is unfunded and settles forward. It is an example of a structured OTC Interest Rate Forward (cell 1 in the unfunded matrix in the Appendix to Chapter 2).

If individual mortgages meet a set of characteristics, they are allowed to be pooled in a trust. The TBA derivative referenced the value of that pool even before the pool was formed and the exact mortgages were known!

This could be done because of the large number of mortgages in the pool and the defined set of characteristics required before the mortgage could be put in the pool which made the pool homogenous.

That is, a mortgage TBA is on a generic pool and exists before the specific mortgages in the pool are announced. The exact mortgages in the pool are To Be Announced (TBA) but the characteristics are homogeneous in coupon, maturity, etc. The settlement of the TBA is forward some number of months (1, 2, etc).

Mortgage TBA's aren't tranched. That is, there is one TBA for each month and type of mortgage pool.

8B2. Derivatives on tranches

An example of OTC forward derivatives on tranches is the CMBX. This derivative moves with the spread of CMBS tranches to Libor.

An example of credit derivatives on tranches is AIG receiving a premium to insure (sell protection) on senior tranches of subprime mortgages. That was one of the contributing factors to 2008 panic. It should be noted that the main problem AIG ran into was the mark to market on the derivative. They were paid little in credit derivative premium and the mark moved dramatically against them and any reserving they did was insufficient. It was fundamentally a liquidity issue.

8B3. Equity derivatives

By far the most common structured equity derivative is the S&P 500 future and S&P options. OTC options on the S&P can go out 10 years! Exchange futures and options on the index go out currently 3-6 months.

Chapter 9. Mathematical Background Necessary to go Deeper into Derivatives.

9A. Basic bond concepts.

9A1. Future Value

Assuming positive rates, $1 invested today is worth more than $1 in the future since the dollar can earn interest over time.

For 1 period, the future $ would be $1 + $1*Interest Rate = $1 * (1 + R). Our second period would be $1 * (1 + R) * (1 + R) = $1 * (1 + R) ^ 2. In general,

Equation 1: FV (T) = PV (0) * (1 + R) ^ T where:

PV (0) = Present Value today (For example $1)

R = Interest Rate per period (For example, 1% per year – a flat yield curve)

^ = Raised to the power of (For example, 2^3=8)

T = Time of Investment in periods (For example, 2 years if R is a yearly rate)

FV (T) = Future Value at time T =$1.0201 = $1 * ((1+.01) ^ 2).

9A2. Present Value

Equation 2: PV (0) = FV (T) / ((1 + R) ^ T) (This follows from Equation 1).

9A3. Discount Factors

Equation 3: DF (0,T) = 1 / ((1 + R) ^ T)

DF (0,T) = The discount factor that takes future cash flows from time T to today (or time 0)

When discount factors are multiplied by the future cash flow at time T (as defined above FV(T)), the present value of that cash flow is obtained. Typically, discount factors are constructed from "par bond" spot rates by the "boot strap" method. The Appendix associated with this section shows these calculations in detail.

9A4. Term Structure

Since discount factors are unique to time and rate earned, a series of discount factors defines the way to discount all future cash flows to today. This series of discount factors is called term structure.

Thus, knowing the term structure, one multiplies each future cash flow by the appropriate discount factor and sums across all cash flows for that investment. Comparing the two sums across investments allows one to pick the higher present value investment.

Term structure is unique to the bond sector. Thus, the term structure for treasury bonds is different than the one for corporate bonds, etc.

Term structure may be calculated by several techniques – boot strap, multiple regression, etc. See associated Appendix for further details.

9A5. Forward Rates

Suppose we want to know if we should buy a five year investment or a two year investment and take the future money and invest in two years for three years?

Define the fair forward rate in two years for three years as 2F3. Assume we know the term structure (discount factors and thus future value factors).

If we start with \$1, \$1 * FV(5) = \$1 * FV(2) * (1 + 2F3) ^ 3. That is, our \$1 should grow in five years as defined by \$1 * FV(5).

It should grow to $1 * FV(2)$ in two years. That amount grown for the next three years is $(1+2F3)$ ^ 3. With FV(5) and FV(2) known, we can solve for the fair forward rate 2F3. See the related Appendix for more details.

9A6. Discount factors vs yield to maturity (YTM).

If one used the term structure concept, the discount factors would be different for each period and calculated through the "boot-strap" procedure mentioned earlier.

Alternatively, one could use the yield to maturity concept to discount cash flows. This uses one yield and is really an average of the discount factors one would get by bootstrapping. The first discount factor would be $1 / (1 + YTM / 2)$ where YTM is annual yield to maturity and would discount the first semi-annual coupon. The next coupon would be discounted by $1 / ((1 + YTM / 2)$ ^ 2). That is, the first discount factor squared (making the numerator 1 *1). Although only one YTM is used, the entire discount factor changes (using the YTM approach) at different times due to raising $(1 + YTM/2)$ to higher powers.

From the future value perspective, you are growing the present value by $(1 + YTM / 2)$. That, in turn, is grown again by $(1 + YTM / 2)$ and that is what causes the squaring.

This YTM concept will not get the same present values of each term created by the cash flows but will get the same sum of the terms (same price). How do we know that? Price is set by market traders and YTM and Discount factors are subsequently solved for. In short, both approaches are really one equation in two unknowns – price and yield.

9A7. Bond Duration

Once you have price and the related yield, how will it change over time? What is the risk due to change in yield/interest rates (and/or credit)?

Interest rate risk is measured by duration for fixed coupon bonds. Like the proverbial elephant, duration can be thought of several ways.

9A7a. Duration as a measure of interest rate risk.

First, it can measure the percentage change in price for a percentage change in YTM. The proof is shown in the related Appendix. That shows:

Equation 4: Macaulay Duration = (dP / (P+A)) / (dI / (I+1))

> **Where dP = price change**
>
> **P+A = price plus accrued**
>
> **dI = interest rate change**
>
> **I = the one interest rate used for discounting YTM**

For example, suppose a 5% YTM bond (I) changes one basis point in yield (dI) and that produces a $0.10 change (dP) in the price of a bond worth $100 in price and $.03 in accrued. We have:

($0.10 / ($100+$.03)) / (.0001 / (1 + .05 / 2)) = 10.25 = Macaulay Duration.

If the bond moves $0.20, the risk is 20.5 – twice the risk.

9A7b. Duration measures holding time for minimum risk

Macaulay Duration is also a measure of the time to hold a bond where, under certain assumptions, changes in interest rates produce a constant total return of the bond over a defined holding period.

If I bought the above bond today and sold it in 10.25 years, two factors determining my worth are in relative balance. The first factor is my reinvested cash flows from now to 10.25 years from now. As rates go up, that amount goes up. The second factor is my price at sale. If rates went up, that value goes down since I would discount my cash flows remaining after 10.25 years at a higher rate. Rates down and my reinvested cash is less at 10.25 years but my price is greater. We have a balance with rates up or down!

Note that this is true for one instantaneous rate move that holds for the entire period. If there were several, the balance is less precise since the reinvested rate would not be linked to the present value rate for future cash flows used for pricing. Never the less, the two amounts are offsetting and can help in risk mitigation.

In summary, I would have a minimum return under the precise assumptions above if I bought the bond "today" and sold the bond at the Macaulay duration. The results are less precise with multiple rate moves over the period. The associated Appendix shows the proof.

9A7c. A second type of Duration - Modified Duration

In practice, modified duration is usually used. It drops the I+1 term and thus is percentage price change for a basis point move in YTM. Thus, Modified duration = Macaulay duration / (1 + (YTM / # of annual compounding periods)). Using the numbers in the above example,

Modified duration * (1 + .05 / 2) = Macaulay duration or

Modified duration = 10 since 10 * 1.025 = 10.25.

9A7d. Duration vs. Maturity

You might think longer maturity bonds are more risky than short maturity bonds so why bother with duration? What does duration add that maturity misses?

The problem with the belief that maturity tells all is that high coupon bonds have less risk than low coupon bonds of the same maturity. This is because the money you spend on high coupon bonds comes back faster (in the way of the high coupons). Thus, it is more "cash-like".

The duration will be lower for high coupon bonds as compared to low when both bonds have the same maturity. Thus, high coupon bonds have less price risk if rates move.

9A7e. Convexity

In the above example, suppose the YTM was 6%. The new Macaulay duration is related to the old duration by convexity. That is

New Duration = Old Duration + (Convexity * Change in Security Interest rates)

For example, suppose at 6% YTM the duration was 10.5. We have convexity = .25 or,

10.5 = 10.25 + .25 * 1

In practice, one usually measures duration across different interest rates to see duration "drift". The "drift" is because of convexity and due to the fact that price and yield are not linearly related. The less the drift, the more stable the duration value with different interest rate levels and the less the convexity.

9B. Basic equity concepts.

Duration measures risk that is not relative to another security but to interest rates. Standard deviation measures risk in the equity world not relative to another security. Both can be said to be measures of "absolute risk".

9B1. Risk measures.

9B1a. The standard deviation of a distribution of numbers.

The standard deviation measures the dispersion of numbers. Find the mean of the set of numbers. Next, take each score minus the mean, square the result, sum each squared difference, divide by n, take the square root.

By squaring each difference from the mean, you are getting the spread regardless of whether it is higher or lower than the mean.

9B1b. Upside/Downside Capture.

Relative risk (risk relative to a benchmark) is usually measured by "upside/downside" capture or beta. If a stock goes up ½ % in a period when the benchmark goes up 1%, the stock captures ½ the upside of the benchmark. If the stock only captures ¼ of the downside, it has favorable upside/downside risk.

9B1c. Beta

In the Capital Asset Pricing Model (CAPM), return of a particular security is a function of the risk free rate and the risk that security has relative to the market.

Imagine getting pairs of monthly returns of the security and market over some period of time. Also get the risk free rate over the same period. Plot the security return on the Y axis and the difference between market return and risk free rate on the X axis.

The slope of the line that best fits the plot is Beta. Thus, Beta tells you how much your security increases in return as the market increases above the risk free rate. If taking risk in your stock has no gain over taking market risk, don't buy the stock.

Now consider the Y value when the X value is 0 (when the market return equals the risk free rate). If the Y value is above the risk free rate, the security has more value than the market. So,

Security return(i) = risk free rate + Beta * (market return(i) – risk free rate)

Where the different "i's" are the different months.

In practice, most measures of Beta are to market return only, not excess return as above. In part, this is because there is disagreement as to what composes the risk free rate. Also, Beta using raw returns is more useful in calculating a hedge ratio. One gets a different hedge ratio using excess returns than when one uses only market returns. The latter does match price changes (see Chapter 13A).

9B2. Return measures.

In bonds, the yield to maturity is the return measure most often used. In equities, the return measure most used is monthly pretax total return. Because the time interval is one month, one usually measures end of the month to end of the month. Any intermediate cash flows are reinvested during the month and contribute to the end of month return. Thus, the numerator is the ending money minus beginning money. The denominator is the beginning money.

For example, a mutual fund has a Net Asset Value (NAV) that is measured this way. It is after fees but before tax.

A second return measure is used in equity other than monthly returns. That is the continuous return measure or "r".

Suppose one compounded every day instead of semi-annually. We get $FV = PV(0) * (1 + (YTM/365))$ ^ 365 where YTM is an annual return. In general, this can be written as $(1 + YTM / n)$ ^ $(n*t)$. The number of compounding periods per year is n and t is the time in years for the return period.

Consider compounding 1 million times a year at 100% YTM. What is the one year future value assuming a PV(0) of $1? We have $1 * (1 + (100\%/1,000,000))$ ^$1,000,000 = 2.71828 = e$^1 where e is the base of the natural logarithms. Since 100% = 1, we have e^r where r is the "close to" continuously compounded rate (1,000,000 times a year). For two years, we square that number.

We have $(e \wedge r) * (e \wedge r) = e \wedge 2r$ or $e \wedge (r*t)$. In short, $1 * e \wedge (r*t)$ = $1 * (1 + (YTM/n)) \wedge (n*t)$ as n approaches infinity.

9C. Performance attribution.

Most total return funds have more than one asset class (for example, stocks and bonds) and multiple securities within an asset class. Are the returns coming from selecting the right asset classes ("top down") or the right securities within an asset class ("bottom up")?

Given a fund and an index and its sub sector returns, one can decide. Let FW(i) be the fund weights in the asset classes and FR(i) be the funds return in those classes. Similarly, the index is IW(i) and IR(i). Since the total return of the fund is the sum of FW(i)* FR(i), subtracting the sum of FW(i) * IR(i) gives the bottom up excess return. That is, keeping asset class weights constant, does the funds return beat the index? If so, the excess comes from security selection. This is the bottom up contribution of the manager.

Next, take the sum of FW(i) * IR(i) minus IW(i) * IR(i). Keeping returns of the asset classes fixed by using the index returns, are the returns better using the funds weights as compared to the index? This is the top down contribution of the manager.

Note that the sum of top down and bottom up equals fund return minus index return or fund excess return. This is also called alpha.

See the example for this section in the Appendix.

9D. Option Pricing

There are two ways to present option pricing – open and closed form.

9D1. Open form pricing

9D1a. The Arbitrage Argument (William F. Sharpe, Investments, Prentice Hall, Inc., 1978, pages 366-373).

Since owning an asset makes you money as prices go up but selling a call costs you money, options can hedge assets when used in some proportion (hedge ratio). That is, they can make you have the same ending worth regardless of what the market does in the future.

Two steps solve this problem. First, find the hedge ratio that gives the same ending dollars assuming either of the two scenarios occurred. Second, present value that single worth to today.

The associated Appendix shows an example.

Suppose you bought a call instead of selling it. The change would be the max terms and C0 would be positive. Following through the math, the hedge ratio "h" would be negative. You would have to short the asset if you bought the calls.

You could also buy a put. The put payoff equation would be

$$h * P1 + MAX(K - P1,0) = h * P2 + MAX(K - P2,0)$$

instead of the call equation using MAX(P-K,0). It is left to the reader to check that buying a put hedges you and selling makes you short the asset (because both MAX terms would have a negative sign in front).

There are six fundamental values in option pricing. What are they?

1. Dividend yield is integrated into the value of the asset. The original expression assumed 0 dividends but one can incorporate them into the price P0, P1 or P2 terms.

2. Spot Price. This is really P0 and can have accrued interest (if bonds) in P0 as can P1 and P2.

3. Strike. This is the K term.

4. Volatility. This creates the 101 or 99 values of P1 and P2.

5. Rate to present value the two identical ending values. This is the r in the 1+r term.

6. Time. This affects the P1and P2 prices and the appropriate rate to present value the ending values.

It is important to note that options priced this way are not subject to the expected mean growth of the asset in the future. Let us assume we think the asset could grow to .8% in the future one period. Since we have the asset either at 101 or 99, we have different probabilities of these two states. In general:

$$P * 101 + (1-P) * 99 = 100.8, \quad P = 0.9.$$

The expectation of a 0.8% return (starting price 100) causes us to weight the scenarios this way.

The reason these probabilities change expectations but not the call price is that the ending values of the hedged portfolios are identical. Said differently, if two outcomes are the same number, weighting them by various weights that all sum to 1 still give you that number!

In the example in the Appendix, we have in step1; 49.5=49.5.

Thus, Step 2 is always present valuing back 49.5 regardless of the probability weights of the two scenarios. Thus, the call price will be the same regardless of different expectations of the asset return.

9D1b. Single period but more than two outcomes

The above approach assumed only two outcomes and that the ending period was at option expiration. What if we want many ending values (but the ending values are still only at option expiration)?

Pricing an option that expires at some time in the future using many ending values involves the following steps:

First, calculate the forward price. That is the mean of a distribution of prices that might happen in the future. The forward date for the forward price is expiration of the forward/option.

Second, assume a shape of the distribution about that mean (symmetric and normal - bell-shaped?).

Third, set the spread of that distribution (implied volatility) defining the width of the range of possible future forward prices.

Fourth, define what the option would pay at each price in the future. Since you assumed a distribution in step 2, these payoffs have an associated probability.

Fifth, present value the payoffs to today (see background in this section on present value) and multiply by the associated probability.

Finally, sum the results across all potential forward prices. That is the worth of the option.

See the Appendix for this section.

9D1c. The Binomial Approach (John C. Cox and Mark Rubinstein, Options Markets, Prentice-Hall, Inc., 1985, 168-179)

The advantage of these approaches (there is more than just one iterative approach) is that we have multiple periods and we can value prior to expiration. In fact, if we make the steps small enough, we approach the calculus involved in Black-Scholes.

Although there are several approaches, we will focus on one to see this convergence.

First, realize we can replicate a call on a stock by mixing different proportions of long stock and long riskless bond in a portfolio. If the stock price is far above the call strike, our position is all stock. Our hedge ratio is 1. Both the call and our "replicating portfolio" move with the stock market. If the stock price is far below the strike, we are all in cash. We hold no stock. Our replicating portfolio is all cash and doesn't move with the market which matches our out of the money call.

Our replicating portfolio of stock and bond must match the call in both up and down markets. It is thus different than the arbitrage approach. In the replicating approach, the values in the two states are the values of the call and are thus different from each other. In the arbitrage approach, the values in the two states are the same- the "hedge" has created two ending states indifferent to the market.

Cox and Rubinstein (1985) presented the analysis shown in the Appendix. The result of this so called "replicating portfolio" approach is that one can create a binomial tree of results and depending on how small the steps are in time, one can replicate the continuous Black-Scholes solution.

The Appendix first starts with a three period option. The call price obtained is $0.75. Part 3 of the Appendix says the binomial approach estimates it to be $1.89. Why the discrepancy?

The answer is too few steps.

Consider the thirty day option example in the Appendix. The price of the option is $2.217 per $100 of stock value. This is calculated using the binomial approach to calculate the probability of 1 up, two ups, etc. Each probability is multiplied by the terminal value of the call since the terminal stock price is known by the number of ups and the probability of an up "P".

Summing those products and present valuing them gives the call price of $2.217.

9D2. Closed form pricing

We will treat Black-Scholes in more detail in the next chapter. Here, we simply want to state the equation and fill in the numbers to get a value. This will show the binomial and Black-Scholes will give the same answer when the same assumptions are used.

The "classic" Black-Scholes equation has no dividends and has five variables.

1. Stock Price Today = 100
2. Time from "today" to option expiry expressed in years = 30/365
3. The "riskless" interest rate over the period expressed annually = .01 or 1%
4. The strike price of the call = 100 (an at the money call)
5. The implied volatility = .19 or 19%

The Appendix shows that "plugging" in these values results in $2.21 for the call premium or price.

Except for implied volatility, it should be clear that all of the values are the same. So, how does one relate implied volatility to the binomial?

First, we need to understand how volatility grows over time in the Black-Scholes world.

The variance of the sum of a set of random variables is the sum of the covariance. Assume a set of monthly returns. If one month's returns tell you nothing about any other month returns, the monthly returns are independent. All covariance "cross terms" vanish and since the covariance of something with itself is variance, one is left with is a series of variances.

~ 74 ~

For example, assume you want an annual estimate of volatility but you only have monthly. You would multiply the monthly variance by 12. Since standard deviation is the square root of variance, **the annual estimate of standard deviation is the monthly standard deviation times the square root of 12.**

Second, how does the discrete binomial approach reflect volatility in the Black-Scholes continuous world?

Clearly, the size of "1+u" and "1+d" is the answer since they drive the asset value. As shown by Cox and Rubinstein (1985, page 199-200), the appropriate relation is $1+u = e$ ^ (vol * sqrt (Time)).In our example, u was over one day, thus 1.01 = 2.71828183 ^ (vol * sqrt (1/365)) .Taking the natural log of both sides, we get Ln (1.01) = vol * .05234239. Thus, vol = .1901 or 19% as used in the Black-Scholes formula.

Chapter 10. Detail View of Black-Scholes Option Pricing.

10A. Basic intuition behind call equation (with no dividends)

C(t) = S(t) *N(d1) – K * e ^ (-r * (T-t)) * N(d2)   (Black-Scholes, no dividends)

Black-Scholes defines the call price as the current price of the stock times N(d1) minus the present value of the strike times N(d2). In other words, the e term simply discounts the strike K from T to t (or today). So we have the present value of the stock times N(d1) minus present value of the strike times N(d2).

To better understand this, consider a call ending in the money in the future. What is the call worth today? Since we give the strike (K) to get the security (S) in the future, it is the present value of S – K. That is, C (t) = PV S(T) – PV (K) = (shall we call them Term 1 – Term 2 ?).

The difference in the two terms would be the correct answer except that S is not a single value but can assume many values in the future as we saw in the previous chapter. This means we must sum all the probability weighted S values to get the expected contribution to the call from Term 1.

To see that this is accomplished by multiplying by N(d1), take the derivative of C(t) with respect to S(t). You get N(d1). That is, N(d1) = dC/dS. Thus, multiplying N(d1) * S(t) would give you the call price if the strike price was negative infinity (dC/dS times S gives you C). Intuitively, a unit change in call price (dC) per unit change in stock price (dS) times total stock price units (S) equals total call units (C).

Now consider Term 2. dC/dK = e ^(-r*(T-t)) * N(d2). Multiplying by K gives the probability weighted value up to K (dC/dK times K gives you the values from negative infinity to K). This is then subtracted. Thus, Term 2 corrects Term 1 for the strike being greater than negative infinity.

10B. Put Intuitions

The associated Appendix shows that puts can be priced using the arbitrage position that owning a call and selling a put is the same as owning a security and borrowing the strike price.

10C. Summary of Chapter 10

The more mathematically inclined will see the other variations of Black-Scholes in the Appendix.

It should be emphasized here that these are descriptive relationships. That is, Black-Scholes is one equation in two unknowns. You tell me option volatility and I will tell you option price knowing strike, time to expiration, etc. Or, you tell me option price and I will tell you volatility.

It is the same with bond yields. There is one equation in two unknowns. You tell me bond price and I will tell you yield.

Thus, in both cases, we are talking about convention. The underlying assumptions are reasonable but they are only assumptions.

As an example of this, options with different strikes many times have different volatilities. Why is this the case if volatility is supposedly a statement of the variation in the distribution of underlying security prices? All strikes point to the same distribution.

The answer is that there is different demand for the currently traded options! Supply and demand ultimately set prices. The correct model of value is defined by whoever is trading the biggest position and where they think value lies. The pricing models simply take those prices and put them in a conceptual framework. They are conventions.

Chapter 11. Detail View of Fixed Income Rate Derivatives (Chapter 5 expanded).

11A. The original rate derivatives – Bonds, Notes, Bills.

In the late 1970's, the first type of modern future developed. These were instruments traded on the Chicago Board of Trade (now CME Group) and allowed for "physical" and cash settlement. That means you could deliver bonds/notes/bills to close out the position or cash payment of the last days margin call (see below).

They were "margined" instruments. Each day, the positions were marked to market and each side started "even". More precisely, the expected one day movement was posted at the beginning of each day. This is how people were comfortable with trading with people they didn't know. That is, trading on the exchange makes the other side relatively unknown to you so to be comfortable, demand upfront money each day to cover one day of price movement.

The equilibrium pricing was discussed previously. That is, spot plus net carry.

But the instruments were priced off a basket of securities, not just one. The idea was to make it difficult to corner the market. If anyone tried to corner the market (get all of one security to control price), another note in the basket would become the note the future priced off of.

The mechanism for this automatic re-pricing was interesting.

Imagine if you delivered any note you were paid such that the yield was (say) 6%. Different notes got different dollar amounts for par because different notes had different coupons, maturities, etc. However, all payments resulted owning 6% yields.

Clearly, market movement could create arbitrage. If the market was 7% yield, buy the note, short the future. During the time between trade and delivery, you are hedged. During the delivery

~ 79 ~

period, deliver the note to close out the futures position and you make the difference in yields.

What was needed was something that made the whole basket move with the market. That is, let F1 be the price (it's called the futures factor) that makes the yield 6% on note 1. F2 is the second note factor, etc. All these "F's" are prices that, if paid, make all the notes have the same yield. Now, multiply all F's by the futures quote. The futures quote is the number you see on the screen.

Thus, the actual "price" dollars delivered if the first bond was delivered is FQ * F1 (plus accrued note interest) where FQ is the futures quote or number on the screen and F1 is that notes factor for that contract and that month. The closing futures quote slides the basket of "F's" up and down as the market moves.

However, the sliding mechanism created an inequality in the bonds/notes/bills. Price and yield aren't linearly related as the present value section showed. Yield to maturity has squared, cubed, etc terms.

For this and other reasons, one note became cheapest to deliver. One note made the most money if you bought it in the market and delivered it into the future. One note had the highest return between today and note expiration - the highest implied repo rate (IRP). It is movement in the price of this note that defines the futures price. In addition, that note can switch since, you guessed it, price and yield aren't linearly related. See the Appendix associated with this section for an example.

11B. The Eurodollar Future and option(s) – the next major development

Libor stands for the London Inter Bank Offer Rate. The rate banks charge each other to lend money. This can be for any term – overnight, one month, one year, ten years, etc. That is, just like the treasury curve, there is a Libor curve – rates for different maturities.

The futures are a series of three month rates. One rate starts today and ends in three months. A second future starts in three months and ends six months from today. It is thus a forward rate – it starts in the future and ends at some further date in the future.

A six month rate can thus be synthesized. Shorting the "nearby" future and the "deferred" future is shorting a six month rate. If rates go up, you are paid. Note that unless the "nearby" starts tomorrow, this is not the same as shorting a "spot starting" six month rate. The futures are in a series and the nearby may not start tomorrow.

The banks that make up LIBOR and their rating are listed below.

2013 Libor Members		
	Rankings	
Company Name	S&P	Moody's
Barclays Bank PLC	A	A2
Bank of America	A-	Baa2
Bank of Tokyo	A+	Aa3
BNP Paribas	A+	A2
Citibank NA	A	A3
Credit Agricole CIB	A	A2
Credit Suisse	A	A1
Deutsche Bank AG	A	A2
HSBC	AA-	Aa3
JP Morgan Chase	A	A2
Lloyds Banking Group	A	A3
Rabobank	AA-	Aa2
Royal Bank of Canada	AA-	Aa3
Societe Generale	A	A2
Sumitomo Mitsui Banking Corporation	A+	Aa3

2013 Libor Members, Cont'd		
	Rankings	
Company Name	S&P	Moody's
The Norinchukin Bank	A+	A1
The Royal Bank of Scotland	A-	Baa1
UBS AG	A	A2
Total Companies= 18		
Rankings as of 9/20/2013		

11C. Interest Rate Swaps and "swaptions"

These derivatives were created when Eurodollar futures were created. In fact, shorting the two futures mentioned above is like receiving floating and paying fixed on a six month swap. If you do the futures trade, you receive margin money as rates go up. If you do a swap, the cash flow occurs at the re-pricing date in three months. Both derivatives are sensitive to the same yields on the Libor curve.

Another way to think about a swap is that it is the same as borrowing to buy a security. If you borrow and buy, you receive fixed (the coupon) and pay floating (the borrowing). The major difference is a security has you receive par at the end and the fixed leg of the swap has no par (nor does the floating leg).

This difference goes away when one realizes that the par you receive at the end from the security must be paid to close out the borrowing when one does the securities transaction. The net is $100 in and $100 out at the end of the leveraged securities trade. The net of the securities transaction is like the net of the fixed and floating legs of the swap. In both cases, worth fluctuates depending on the value of a fixed rate and there is no par at the end.

Given that, one realizes that options on swaps are identical to options on fixed rate securities. If the swap the option is on starts at option expiration, the floating leg never sets and is always at market. Thus, the worth is driven by the difference between the fixed rate in the market and the strike. This is the same for options on fixed rate securities (but not caps). See the Appendix.

Chapter 12. Detail View of Credit Derivatives (Chapter 6 expanded).

12A. More Detail on Single Name Pricing

As stated in the basic credit derivative chapter, the pricing intuition is probability of survival * credit derivative premium = probability of default * loss if default. In that chapter, we calculated one period survival to be .9836 using simplistic assumptions. This might or might not be the same probability as the rating agency default tables.

What about multiple periods?

First, we need to add a discount factor. Premiums are actually paid quarterly, but for simplicity, assume yearly. Thus, we need to bring these payments back to today's dollars.

Now, suppose we have n periods. Let

$P(0,n)$ = the credit derivative premium for n years

$DF(0,n)$ = the discount factor for n years to today

R = assumed recovery of defaulted bond; assume $40 per $100 notional

$PS(0,n)$ = probability of survival from today to n years

For no arbitrage, we have to satisfy that the sellers expected payout is equal to the buyers for the n periods. We have:

	Seller's money	/ Buyer's money
Period 1	$P(0,n)*DF(0,1)*PS(0,1)=Term(1)$	$/ = -Term(1)$
Period 2	$P(0,n)*DF(0,2)*PS(0,2)=Term(2)$	$/ = -Term(2)$

.

.

Period (n-1) $P(0,n)*DF(0,n-1)*PS(0,n-1)=Term(n-1)$

$$/ = -Term(n-1)$$

Period n $\quad P(0,n)*DF(0,n)*PS(0,n)=Term(n)$

$$/ = (100-R)*DF(0,n)*(1-PS(0,n))$$

The seller receives premium $P(0,n)$ assuming survival ($PS(0,i)$ for i = 1 to n-1) and for n-1 periods the buyer pays the premium. All cash flows are discounted to today ($DF(0,i)$. On the nth period, default occurs ($1-PS(0,n)$) or not ($PS(0,n)$).

Assuming one has the premiums ($P(0,n)$) for different periods from the credit derivatives market, this allows a "bootstrap process" to get solutions for $PS(0,n)$. One starts at one period, then two, etc.

Note that equilibrium pricing occurs in a three period case only if all three periods occur. If default happens before, say in two periods, the buyer has a windfall profit but has paid too much as compared to only buying two periods of protection.

12B. Standardized pricing

Currently (2014), premiums are standardized. This means, for example, all high grade corporate bonds have 1% premiums. The seller is paid $1 per $100 notional per year. Since there are really different values for different credits, an upfront fee is paid to compensate the buyer or seller so that the uniform premium is fair.

For example, assume a one year case and the premium should be $ .80 for a good credit company. If the buyer premium is $1, they are paid $.20 upfront by the seller for a one year contract. This neglects present valuing.

12C. Solving for other than probability of survival

The above assumed you knew the credit derivative pricing (the premiums for different terms). Thus, we solved for probability of survival much like one solves for yield knowing the price of a bond.

Suppose you wanted to know the distribution of possible premiums assuming different probabilities of survival. You would create a distribution of the probabilities of survival and solve for the premiums.

One could also use Monte Carlo simulation (see a later chapter) but the math would be the same.

12D. Credit derivative indices.

The current investment grade index is 125 names and is equally weighted. Thus, the levels of each credit name are aggregated to arrive at one premium.

There are also tranches on this index. That is, default goes to the lowest tranche, etc. Thus, both the index alone and tranches on the index are currently traded.

Chapter 13. Detail View of the Rest of the Asset Classes – Equity (Public and Private), Commodity, Currency, Real Estate – (Chapter 7 expanded).

13A. Public Equity Alternative Investments

13A1. The Greeks – How option characteristics can change.

Before discussing the Greeks, let's review the inputs to the option pricing model presented previously but add one – dividend yield. We have **(1) Dividend yield/bond coupon, (2) spot price, (3) strike, (4) implied volatility, (5) short term rate, (6) time**. Option prices are also said to be intrinsic + time value. That simply groups the above variables. Intrinsic is defined by spot and strike. All six variables define time value – the fact that the option that has 0 intrinsic is still worth something with time remaining since it could go into the money in the remaining time.

Another way to group these inputs is what defines the forward price and what is unique to options? Forward prices are spot plus net carry which means spot price, dividend yield, short term rate and time define the forward price. Unique to options is strike and volatility. Strike defines what security price starts the present valuing of the outcomes and volatility defines the standard deviation of the forward pricing distribution.

If you have option pricing software, all Greeks can be obtained by changing the above inputs to the pricing software. For example, to measure delta (see below), change the security price and see how that changes the option price. Also, to measure gamma, make security price changes and measure option price changes but at several different security price levels, etc.

The amount of change in the security price (the denominator) should be as small as you can make it and get a "readable" change in the numerator. Said differently, these measures are derivatives in the calculus sense and so really measure the effects of small, instantaneous changes.

The problem with the Greeks, in real life, is that the inputs change in a correlated way, not independently. Thus, matching some Greeks in a hedge does not mean you necessarily have an effective hedge unless you match all of them and that never happens in a hedge since you never go long and short the same thing. That said, matching some of them is better than none. **The major Greeks are:**

Delta = Change in option price / Change in Underlying Security Price (or, USP). For example, if the option price goes from $0.50 to $1.00 when the security price goes from $22 to $23, the delta is ½ [($1.00-$0.50) / ($23-$22)] . Since a put decreases in option premium when the security price goes up, the put delta is negative and the call delta positive. So,

New option price = Old option price + Delta * Change in USP.

Gamma = Change in Delta / Change in USP. So,

New Delta = Old Delta + Gamma * Change in USP.

Theta = Change in Option Price / Change in time. An ATM (At The Money) option is worth something with time to expiration even though the strike equals the underlying price. This is because it could end up being worth something by expiration. This is also called "time value". Note, as mentioned before, employee stock options don't have time value and thus differ from normal options (are worth less). Because of time value, Theta is a measurable value – options change in value over time with nothing else changing. So,

New option price = Old option price + Theta * Change in time.

Vega = Change in Option Price / Change in Implied Volatility. The lower the volatility used to price the option, the less the option price is for both a put and call. Note that implied volatility is to option price as yield is to bond price – knowing one you know the other. As previously stated, all pricing exercises in finance reduce to one equation in two unknowns – price and yield. Knowing one, you know the other but it isn't a unique solution because there isn't a second independent equation! Perhaps this is why we have Guru's! So,

New option price = Old option price + Vega * Change in Implied Volatility.

Rho = Change in Option Price / Change in Interest Rates. This is the most complex of all the Greeks! For example, in equity options, there could be multiple rates that define Rho.

The **first** is current dividend yield. As it is changed, the forward price changes.

If it is a long dated option, the **second** rate is growth of dividend yield.

The **third** rate is the long term rate. Many equity pricing models discount expected future dividends or cash flows and arrive at security price using the long term rate (say, 10 year treasuries plus a spread).

The **fourth** rate is the rate from today to option expiration – the classic input "Short Term Rate". **It is usually this rate that is meant in Rho calculations.** So,

New option price = Old option price + Rho * Change in Short Term Rates

Clearly, the longer the time to expiration, the more the option is sensitive to rates.

13A2. Equity hedge ratios of two funded assets

The goal of all hedge ratios is to match price changes of two securities. If additionally the Greeks are matched, one has reason to believe the price changes will stay matched and the hedge ratio will be more stable than if the Greek's aren't matched.

The alternative to carefully matching the Greeks is to periodically rebalance the hedge. This is the most common approach. In equities, that means either **directly measuring the price changes** over some time period of the two assets **or calculating the price changes** knowing the market value and returns of each.

For example, let

dPn = Asset n price **change** over some time period,

MVn = Market value of Asset n at the beginning of the period,

Rn = Return over some time period of Asset n,

HRn = how much we need of Asset (n) to match the other Asset.

Suppose $dP1$ = $100, $dP2$ = $200. We need twice the current market value ($MV1$) of Asset 1 to match the price change associated with Asset 2 at $MV2$.

$HR1$ = $dP2$ / $dP1$ = 2 (We need twice MV of Asset 1 to match Asset 2).

Since $dPn = MVn * (1 + Rn) - MVn = MVn * Rn$, we have

$$HR1 = MV2*R2 / MV1*R1 = (MV2/MV1) / (R1/R2)$$

Notice that we only need an estimate of R1 relative to R2 over our hedging period. We might simply average monthly returns of the two assets over some time period and take the ratio of the averages to get our estimate of R1/R2. A more sophisticated approach is plotting pairs of returns (say monthly) over some time period (say 5 years) and finding the slope of the best fitting line. If done this way, with Asset1 on the Y axis and Asset2 on the X axis, we have an estimate of "raw" Beta or R Beta(1 to 2).

In the mathematical chapter, we learned that in CAPM, the beta is calculated using EXCESS returns. That is, raw returns minus the risk free rate. That is clearly not R1/R2. **The Appendix of this section shows the following. Only if beta is raw return of market on the X axis and raw return of an asset on the Y axis does one get the following equation (widely used). It describes how much asset 1 to match price changes of asset 2.**

$$HR1 = (MV2 / MV1) / (R1 / R2) = (MV2 / MV1) / \text{Beta (1 to 2)}$$

If how much asset 2 relative to asset 1 to create equal price change is required, we clearly have the inverse, or

$$HR2 = \text{Beta (1 to 2)} / (MV2 / MV1)$$

In both these equations, Beta (1 to 2) means the slope of the plot of asset 1 returns on the Y axis and asset 2 returns on the x axis).

The Appendix gives detail for unfunded assets like futures.

13B. Private Equity Alternative Investments.

In the overview chapter, we discussed how managers invest in deals and how investors are paid. The question addressed here is what is the investors return?

In mutual funds, the answer is relatively simple. All money is put in at one time and any asset not sold is marked to market. Thus, the return is distributed cash plus liquidation of fund value or NAV.

We suggest that in private equity, marks on unrealized deals should not be used since they are not reliable. After all, this is private equity and the deals aren't publically traded.

Thus, two IRR's should be calculated. The first should be capital invested and capital distributed to the investor (after management fees and carried interest). The second IRR should include unrealized marks for each period in addition to actual distributions as above.

Due to the simplicity of this approach, we do not include numerical examples but believe success should be measured by convergence of these two returns over time.

Two final issues.

First, we suggest the investor discusses the base of the management fee calculations with the fund manager. The convention is that the percentage (perhaps 2%) is on cumulative "called down" capital. What if the investment has matured? Should the investor pay the manager for deals "dead and gone" as well as current deals? The sum of the two is the current convention.

Another discussion is exactly how is "carried interest" calculated? It is supposed to represent an incentive to the manager for exceptional performance. But suppose performance is exceptional one year and not the next? It would seem some of the money paid should be returned to the investor if performance is not exceptional but the prudent investor should clarify that with the manager.

13C. Commodity Alternative Investments

In the overview of commodities we did in the basic level treatment chapter, we noted that commodity carry had one component (cost) and that normal forward pricing should therefore increase over time. This is called "contango". Contango would logically seem the "normal" situation since one has to be compensated for bearing the storage cost over time and thus one wants a higher forward price.

The difficulty in any formal analysis is assessing that cost. It can be very different for different firms in the same business and certainly across businesses. For this reason, commodities are very technical – it depends on who is in the market and rumors of supply and demand.

The market also is a very "short dated" forward market. One is only able to establish typically one to three month forward positions in any size at one point in time. Thus, hedgers need to roll contracts. Of course, rolling with uncertain levels makes this not a hedger's market but a speculators market.

Much is made of the diversification value of commodities. These comparisons are usually made to a particular asset – for example stocks. Commodities might reduce stock risk but do they do it more efficiently than (say) blending stocks with bonds and cash or hedging stocks slightly? These alternatives (so to speak) might be more efficient than adding commodities to one's portfolio.

13D. Currency Alternative Investments

13D1. The trade that defines "fair value"

As previously stated, the currency markets are theoretically bounded by the basic trade of investing in a security that has the currency and rate of country A vs taking the same amount of currency of country A, (1) spot converting to country B currency, (2) investing in B's security and (3) doing a forward to bring the B currency back to currency A. These two operations should result in the same amount of money in the end. This trade is very heavily arbitraged and the equality holds for **short dated** instruments.

The equality holds surprisingly well with longer dated instruments (say 10 year notes). This trade is usually not executed with a series of forwards but with full currency swaps (swapping all cash flows).

The hedged trade has four "legs". Buy foreign bond (receiving fixed foreign coupons and par), borrow to do it (pay foreign floating rates), pay foreign fixed rates in a swap, receive foreign floating rates.

The inefficiencies in currency trades come when one needs to get out of the trade before the maturity of the rate security. For example, you set up the four legged trade and need to get out after two years. The majority of trades are banks hedging their loan book and your maturity may not match their needs. The markets then can get wide (inefficient). You get in but may have trouble getting out early.

13D2. Basket Trades

An example of a trade frequently done in currency is a basket trade. A series of forwards of different currencies are shorted relative to another currency. It is anticipated that the long currency will appreciate relative to the basket and/or the convergence of the forwards you earn is more than the convergence you pay.

13D3. Yen Carry Trade

Another popular trade was to borrow yen, spot convert to USD, buy high yielding USD note. The yen rates were so low that one earned the spread between the USD note and the yen debt. Of course, if the yen appreciated, you might suffer a loss because the USD you got from selling the note gave you too little yen to repay the yen borrowing.

13D4. The Aussie, Brazilian Real Carry Trade

Australia is a major exporter of coal, wool and other commodities. Thus this trade is perhaps a more focused version of the Yen Carry Trade mentioned above. Owning the Aussie note allows you to win two ways – either the Australian dollar strengthens due to commodity prices going up or the economy improving in general. That said, Japan is a major importer of oil so maybe it is a bit focused also? Maybe one does the note part of the carry trade 50% Australia, 50% Japan and gets a partial commodity hedge?

13E. Real Estate Alternative Investments

13E1. Whole Loan deals

Real Estate "whole loan" lending simply means the lender lends to the borrower and doesn't sell the loan into a structure. They keep the loan and assume credit/default risk themselves.

Assume one buys a shopping complex. The stores pay lease payments. Subtracting expenses from lease payments gives NOI (net operating income). Subtracting depreciation and interest paid on debt gives taxable income and applying the tax rate gives resulting tax payments.

The after tax cash flow is NOI minus P&I debt payments minus taxes as calculated above. This after tax cash flow is what you get prior to sale of the property.

The sales price can be estimated using "cap rate". The annual NOI / property price = cap rate. Thus, at purchase, the cap rate is known. Projecting cap rate forward (at some growth rate) is the art of real estate investing. With NOI also projected forward, sales price can be estimated by dividing projected NOI / projected cap rate. Thus, we can estimate "carry" and capital gains.

13E2. Structured Real Estate

When the lender sells the loans into a structure, they are repaid what they lent immediately and are free to lend again. This "packaging" of residential and commercial loans is more typical than keeping the whole loan on the books. Structured assets are the topic of the next Chapter.

Chapter 14. Detail View of Structured Paper (Chapter 8 expanded).

This Chapter has two Appendices. In Appendix A&B, we present a generic analysis of a structure assuming the asset in the pool is a fixed rate loan. This analysis is divided into two parts, the asset pool and one of the note tranches. In Appendix C, we present detailed mathematics associated with Appendix A&B.

14A. Asset Pool

Following Appendix 14A&B, the asset pool has a legal final maturity. This is the last maturity of all loans in the pool. That legal final is 84 months from "as of date" – the date of the analysis. The trust is liquidated before or near that legal final date depending on how fast the loans are repaid.

Next is the Weighted Average Maturity (WAM). This is often reported in the trust report that the trustee prepares monthly. It is the weighted (by current outstanding balance) maturity of the loans in months. This weighting is just taking into account maturity. Loans with the same maturities but different cash flows would have the same number. Only the maturity matters, not the interim cash flows.

Next is the Initial balance of the pool – the aggregate of all outstanding balances. This (as well as all numbers) is at an "as of date" since not all loans need start on the same date. Some loans are "aged". Next is servicing. This is the money the servicer gets because they collect the money from the loans, work out bad loans, etc. In general, they process the cash flows from the borrowers.

Next is initial prepayment expressed as a CPR (Conditional Prepayment Rate). This is the percentage of principal payment **beyond** scheduled principal payment. It is expressed annually. If expressed monthly, it is called SMM (Single Monthly Mortality). Appendix C shows the relation between CPR and SMM. Going from one to the other is analogous to going from annual yield to monthly yield.

Recovery is the percentage of default that is repaid.

Weighted Average Life is next. Instead of just maturity, this statistic sums the product of time from today times any principal cash flow across the pool of mortgages. It divides by the outstanding principal of the pool at as of date.

We now describe the columns. Column 2 defines the weighted average coupon (WAC) of the pool. It is like the other statistics – gross coupon is weighted by outstanding balance across the mortgages in the pool. It is a vector since aging should make the higher coupon mortgages prepay first (as well as default first). Thus, the pool should have a downward "taper" to WAC.

Column 3 defines CPR as a vector. Not only do single mortgages prepay with different rates as they age, but also pools certainly prepay differently as the fast payers die out, etc. Thus, it is best to have loan "tapes". That is, loan by loan data. Ideally, each loan would be analyzed and an aggregate CPR would be created.

Deferment is next in Column 4. This is where a borrower has borrowed but is not paying. They are not in default. An example would be a student loan for education. They started to pay but went back to school and are allowed to defer payments. The interest is capitalized (added to the balance due) when the loan is in deferment. Percent Deferred per period is quoted in Column 4.

Next we have default. Column 5 assumes each period percent default occurs at the beginning of the period and some recovery is assumed at the end of the period. In reality we might assume a much longer time period for recovery. Of course, default reduces the principal in the pool. No interest is capitalized. Default is expressed per period as a percent (.1 = a tenth of 1%)..

Column 6 is the pool balance at the end of the period. It is the **sum** of

1. this period balance (8) after default (which occurs at the beginning of the period)

2. plus this period capitalized interest (13)
3. plus this period recovery (18)
4. minus total principal that flows to the tranches (19).

Adding recovery (18) cancels the recovery subtracted in (19). Said differently, recovery comes in as a cash flow to the pool but goes out to the tranches thus gross default defines the reduction in pool principal without including recovery.

Column 7 simply applies the period default to the prior end of period balance. Column 8 is the pool balance net (subtracting out) of default. Column 9 applies the WAC to the balance in column 8. The WAC is quoted annually so it must be divided by 12.

Column 10 defines the amount taken by the servicer and column 11 gives net interest (9-10).

Column 12 reduces column 11 by the percentage of period deferment. It is column 11 times (1 - % deferment). The difference between columns 11 and 12 is Column 13. Column 13 defines the interest added to the loan balance (Capitalized Interest) since deferment is not forgiveness – you must pay, just later.

Column 15 starts the principal calculations. This is each month's amount of principal due after default. See Appendix 14C for the full equation. This is the formula behind the PMT function in Excel except that PMT includes interest. Thus, use PMT and subtract out interest (Loan Balance (i) * WAC(i) / 1200) to get principal only.

Column 16 is the unscheduled principal due after default. It is the CPR applied to the balance of the pool remaining after Column 15. Again see Appendix 14C for further details.

Column 17 would be the sum of 15 and 16 except for deferment. Thus, Column 17 is the sum times the percent deferment and expressed as a negative number since it decreases principal paid.

Column 18 is the recovery assumed to be received at the end of the month from the beginning month default. As stated before, this could be delayed more as suited.

Column 19 is the sum of columns 15 – 18. It is the total principal available to distribute to the tranches. Column 20 adds interest (column 12) to get principal and interest available to the tranches. In most structures, principal and interest are separated and not commingled as the money flows to the tranches.

Column 21 is the remaining Principal balance of the pool. It is the same as Column 6. It is presented as a convenient way to keep track of the tranche flows which are next.

14B. Note Tranches

As stated previously, there are two typical ways the pool cash flows go to the tranches – waterfall and pro-rata. In both structures, interest is paid to all tranches in proportion to their par.

In waterfall, there is a sequence from one tranche to the next in principal. Thus, the senior tranche "faces" the entire pool until it is paid off (or "exhausted"), then the next tranche, etc. Default reduces the pool and lowest (equity) tranche. Recovery and prepayment flow to the top tranche.

In pro-rata, principal is divided between all tranches in proportion to their par. That is, all tranches pay down at once.

Column 24 assumes a waterfall structure. The tranche starts paying when the pool balance is down to $800,000. It is thus not the top tranche but somewhere in the middle ("mezzanine"). It is "exhausted" at a pool balance of $700,000. That is, it is $100,000 par note or tranche. It is assumed to have floating interest at 1 month Libor plus a spread of 100 basis points (1%). Appendix 14C presents the detailed calculations.

The logic of column 24 is as follows. As long as the pool balance is above the exhaustion of the tranche more than the width, the tranche isn't active. The width stays untouched. As soon as the pool balance is in the active range, the tranche width shrinks 1:1 with the pool- the tranche pays off. Below exhaustion, the tranche width stays 0.

Appendix 14C also shows how to look at tranche par as a put spread. The premium of the put spread is tranche width and the strikes of the two puts are at insertion and exhaustion.

Chapter 15. Managing Alternatives – Efficient Frontiers and Monte Carlo Simulation.

15A. Efficient Frontiers

This is a mathematical solution to the question "if I can weight different assets in a group, what is the best weighting (gives the highest expected return) for a given level of risk"?

One can imagine trying a variety of weights for each asset (w1,w2, etc) and getting the resultant return and risk of the mixture. Of course, that would be cumbersome.

The aggregate return is the weighted sum of the individual returns. That is,

Aggregate return = W1*R1 + W2*R2 + W3*R3 +   +Wn*Rn [1]

Where R1 etc is the expected return of asset 1 over some time period, R2 is the second asset return over the same period, etc.

15A1. What is the aggregate risk?

Consider two variables and define risk as standard deviation. It is tempting to assume the aggregate risk is the weighted standard deviations.

The problem is that the above assumes the variables are independent. If one variable is the exact opposite of the other, the two would truly have no risk if equally weighted but that would not be the result if you equally weight each standard deviation.

For two (or n) variables, the square root of the weighted sum of the covariances is the correct answer. That is,

Variance of n variables = Var =   {sum (i=1,n) sum (j=1,n)} [W(i) * W(j) * Covar (i,j)]   [2]

Aggregate Risk = Std Dev = Square Root of Var

The Appendix gives a numerical example.

15A2. But how do we get an efficient frontier?

Given the above arithmetic in section A1, we simply need a linear program such as supplied in Excel Solver. That is, maximize the weighted sum of the returns (equation [1]) and constrain the aggregate risk (equation [2]) to some range. Also, make the sum of the weights 1 in order to be fully invested and each weight greater than zero (to avoid short selling).

Record the weights for that range of risk and set another range on the risk and get the new weights and weighted return of the Solver solution.

15B. Monte Carlo Solutions

The technique described above solves for a set of return / risk solutions all over one period. Suppose you want to find out what that solution becomes over time? Or, suppose you want to have some set of assumptions good for some period and a different set of assumptions for another? Monte Carlo can do all these things and many others. For this reason, it is called "open form option pricing" when used to price options or just "open form" when doing other pricing.

Monte Carlo modeling usually involves assuming a variable has some distribution over time that has at least a mean and standard deviation. The usual assumption is that the distribution is normal (if option pricing, price is log normal). For simplicity, always use returns and assume they are normally distributed.

Thus, as we go out in time, the mean drifts as a function of time. For any given time (from start) the actual observations are randomly distributed about that drifted mean.

If we make the mean drift by net carry (see forward pricing) and the variance of the distribution at a point of time be defined by implied volatility, we say the scenarios are calibrated to the capital markets. The implications of this are:

1. Option values at expiration can be present valued and one gets Black-Scholes pricing.

2. The scenarios are arbitrage free. That is, one can't have two positions of equivalent risk and make more money in one position as compared to the other.

3. The scenarios are risk neutral. This means all assets earn the financing rate if sold at the forward price. To see this, consider owning the asset and assume selling it at the forward price (using the scenario prices). We have:

Money earned = Forward Price – Spot Price + Dividend/Coupon

Money earned = (Spot Price + Financing - Dividend/Coupon) – Spot Price + Dividend/Coupon = Financing

That is, we would earn the financing rate. Assuming we did a leveraged transaction that cost the financing rate, we earn 0.

Another way to say this is the following. Buying an asset and hedging yourself by selling a forward should only earn the financing rate. If you hedge yourself, you are indifferent to the market as you are if you simply own cash.

Thus, own asset and sell a future/forward = Own cash

Or, own asset = Own cash and buy a future/forward. This says you can create bonds using forwards and cash. A correctly calibrated set of scenarios makes these two trades earn the same money.

In summary, Monte Carlo scenarios must be made to be arbitrage free if used to currently price an asset that has traded forwards. The scenarios must be normally distributed at any point in time with the mean being the forward price. The standard deviation is the implied volatility. If this is done, all equivalent risk positions earn the same. For example, owning cash and futures is the same as owning the asset associated with the future.

Expectations can be used in Monte Carlo simulations but they answer a different question than pricing. That question is "what might I earn over time assuming my personal scenarios?" One's expectation is that one will experience something different than the current set of forwards over time. One's expectation is different than consensus of people actually trading the asset.

For example, assume one thinks the "capital markets" forwards are too low. One expects the means of the distribution to be higher and makes them higher in their Monte Carlo simulations. One could now compare today's price with the present value of one's future expectations gotten through the Monte Carlo. However, that higher value using expectations is not the price, by definition. It is simply your guess as to worth and not an observable price in the capital markets. One can't lock in that higher gain using capital markets instruments since they assume forwards.

The inconsistency is that you are using your expectation on what you own but if you hedge what you own in the capital markets, those instruments assume different scenarios – the forwards. There would be two different views of the world at the same time if one thought expectations should be associated with pricing.

See the Appendix for an example of Monte Carlo pricing using returns to grow asset values.

Chapter 16. Legal and Regulatory Issues in Alternatives (including Dodd-Frank).

Due to 2008 and the resulting strain on the market, legislation (the Dodd-Frank Act) was passed to attempt to prevent future financial meltdowns. The culprits were and are still believed to be leverage in the OTC market and transparency.

OTC leverage was excessive since once a trade occurred, margining in the OTC market often didn't occur. Although a document was in place to define margining (The CSA Annex to the ISDA), few margin calls were actually made prior to 2008. That is, if the derivative "mark to market" went one person's way, they often didn't ask for assets from the other party to "reset to zero." It was a private placement "gentleman's" market. Dealers didn't call dealers, dealers didn't call good customers (they traded a lot) and good customers didn't call dealers (customers wanted good prices).

Transparency was also lacking. Two people simply did the trade on the phone. One quarter later, it might show up on the financials.

Thus, it is perhaps natural that the current thought seems to be to make the OTC market like the exchange market. First, have OTC exchanges instead of allowing private transactions on the phone. Thus, have OTC execution occur electronically with multiple observable bids from different exchange dealers (as the exchange seems to be drifting to also). Second, enforce margining like the Exchange derivatives markets. Thus, have one day of potential derivative price movement posted at the beginning of the trading day and remark the next day.

Some issues with this approach include (a) too big to fail, (b) derivatives in structured paper, (c) fraud.

The "too big to fail" issue is that forming exchanges means having exchange members. They trade with each other and stand for each other. So suppose one member goes down. The others have to stand in and cover the problem. Thus, exchanges create too big to fail since they link all members together.

The "derivatives in structured paper" issue is that the rules only cover outright derivative trades. What if the derivative is put in structured paper? For example, suppose the original trade is a single name credit default swap referencing party A. The dealer sells protection. If A defaults, the dealer pays. The dealer inserts this credit default swap into a pool and tranches the resulting cash flow from the credit derivative premium. They make money on issuing the new structured set of notes and are no longer "on the hook" to pay if default. The investor in the notes now has the credit risk.

Thus, a dealer could simply write as many of these derivatives as they like and not be at risk. The problem here is that the ultimate risk taker (the investor) is not at the "deal table" when the security is created. The dealer is - they are responsible for creating the derivative and the structured paper. The trustee is – they are mainly a paying and reporting agent. The rating agency is – they run their models and give credit ratings to the notes. The investor is absent and shown the notes by the dealer. This allows the potential for fraud.

Perhaps one solution is to pay the rating agencies and dealer based on performance. Currently, the dealer and rating agency are both paid an upfront fee when the structured paper is sold to investors regardless of subsequent performance of the paper. An alternative is to pay some of the fees to the agency and dealer over time. If the paper behaves as the ratings implied (AAA doesn't default), the agency and dealer get some fees upfront and the rest at note maturity. Otherwise, the accruing part of the dealer and agency fee is paid to the investor at note maturity.

Chapter 17. Accounting and Tax Issues in Alternatives.

Most descriptions of profit and loss in derivative trades are pretax and ignore accounting. So, for example, the profit of buying a call at expiration is usually stated to be max(S-K, 0). That is, if the security price (S) is greater than the strike (K), the profit is S-K. If not, 0 since the call expires worthless.

This ignores the entire time between purchase, holding the security and sale. That is what **GAAP** accounting is all about. It states rules defining how to value assets and liabilities between purchase and sale.

Any derivative purchase involves a small outlay of cash. Thus, at purchase, the balance sheet effect is cash is reduced and the asset is placed on the books. Net, there is no change in assets assuming the value is the cash expended. Assume the derivative becomes more valuable the next reporting period (in a quarter?). In general, the derivative change is reported in earnings unless it is deemed hedging another asset. If hedging, both the mark on the derivative and the security hedged flows through earnings. They can offset each other but if not perfectly, there is an effect on earnings.

Derivatives are thus marked through earnings whether hedging or not. This differs from securities. The mark on securities purchased "alone" flows through the surplus account on the balance sheet.

Earnings are far more "under the microscope" than changes in surplus. For this reason, it seems derivatives are at a disadvantage as compared to securities. But are they? What about the magic of putting derivatives in a pool and making them structured paper as described above. Suddenly, the mark of the structured paper backed by derivatives is away from earnings and back on the balance sheet!

It can get even better. Does the mark even have to go on the balance sheet? Suppose the dealer puts credit default swaps in a trust and an investor pays money to own the tranches of the trust.

You get a fee as the manager but you also buy some of the lower tranches of the issuance. Now, depending on the tranches you might own, their size and the risk assigned by the rating agency, there may be no mark on your tranches at all. The investment is off your balance sheet (and onto the investors) if your risk is "de minimis".

The general point is that making individual derivative trades marked to market is not really a safeguard. Not if one can securitize derivatives or structured paper that is backed by derivatives. Thus, it is tempting to suggest that the test of marking to market through earnings should be whether the paper can default because it is backed by risky assets like derivatives. If the major risk is derivatives related, mark the paper through earnings regardless of whether it meets other "safe harbor / de minimis" tests.

The above were GAAP accounting considerations. Statutory (or STAT) is insurance accounting. Assets are carried at amortized cost. Thus, if a bond cost $101, has a life of ten years and is expected to mature at par (or $100), $.10 is written off per year in earnings and surplus unless it is impaired (deemed permanently devalued). At that point, a loss is recognized in earnings and hence surplus.

STAT has no concept of hedging. This generally means that under STAT accounting, one amortizes the derivative cost over time. This is interesting since derivatives are levered (cost little to begin with).

Tax accounting for derivatives requires one to identify character and timing for taxation on the day of the trade. Timing means you are fully taxed (a) "upfront", (b) over time or (c) at the end of the trade. Character means is the transaction Capital or Ordinary? Finally, the "holding period" of the transaction alters the rate paid.

Capital means profit from asset sales. Ordinary means wages, salaries, tips, etc. The concept is that Capital gains/losses are from "things" that help produce "Ordinary" income.

Both Capital and Ordinary can be considered either long term or short term depending on the "holding period" or time from trade to sale of the derivative. Of the four resulting cases, the most favorable (lowest tax rate) for individual investors is long term (greater than one year) capital transactions. Currently (late 2013), corporations are taxed at the same rate (35%) for both Capital and Ordinary.

Even though corporations are taxed at the same rate for Capital and Ordinary, they are separate "buckets". Losses of one character cannot be offset by gains of another character.

If one experiences a loss in one year (a Net Operating Loss or NOL), the amount of the loss you take is affected by character of the gain you net with the loss. If the NOL is taken against a Capital gain, the loss is limited but if against an Ordinary gain it is not.

Chapter 18. Case Studies using Alternatives

18A. Fixed Income Rates

18A1. Hedging a future debt issuance

A corporate treasurer thinks rates are low today and will go up in the future. Since they borrow, this will cost more money in the future. How can they protect themselves?

They could issue today and lock in the rate of borrowing. But, suppose they don't need the money? They would be paying interest on money they didn't need.

Better, they could "short" a forward. This could be on an Exchange (like the CBOT) or over the counter. If on the exchange, the forward is called a future.

Assume the issuance is 50 million of a fixed rate note 10 years to maturity. The most likely hedging candidates are:

1. Short a 10 year note future.

If the future approach is chosen, one needs to determine the cheapest to deliver note (call a finance professional or use software). Change the yield on the note a basis point and divide the price difference by the futures factor for that note and contract month. The result is the price change the future should make for a basis point change in yield. Since that change is for $100 par and the contract is $100,000 par, multiply by 1,000. Divide that into the issuance price change for a basis point change in yield and you have the number of contracts.

The cost is the gross basis - see the Appendix for Chapter 11 for details.

2. Reverse in a security

In a reverse, you fix the price today that you will sell a security you own in the future. If the market price goes lower in the future, you make money (sold high and bought low).

The hedge ratio is price change in the security reversed vs issuance price change (or, whatever you are hedging).

It should be noted that the repo and reverse markets are currently shrinking due to banks wanting to conserve capital. That is, the trade requires capital since it extends credit to the institution.

3. Pay fixed for ten years and receive floating on a forward starting swap.

If the swap approach is taken, start it in the future when the issuance is expected. Thus, the floating leg is irrelevant – the floating rates are at market throughout the hedge since they are never fixed.

To calculate a hedge ratio, take the ratio of change in price of issuance to that of the swap. The change in price of the swap is a function of the fixed rate – treat it like a note.

The cost of swap hedging is the fact that the forward will become "spot" over time. Thus, the fixed rate difference between the spot and forward rate of the swap is the cost in yield.

The swap is probably the best hedging tool since it has a spread to treasuries as a corporate issuance would also have. The futures are treasury based and the reverse is a specific issue.

18A2. The value of "Assignment"

During the S & L crisis of the late 1980s, and more recently the financial crisis of 2008, there were a high number of bank failures. The Federal Deposit Insurance Corporation (FDIC) was responsible for taking over failed banks during these two crises and it inherited a portfolio of illiquid assets. Some of these assets were derivative securities i.e. interest rate swaps, interest rate caps and/or floors.

These OTC derivatives were not liquid (could not be unwound) if the failed bank owed money to a non-failed (bigger) counterparty. These bigger institutions did not fail in the 2008 crisis (another branch of the government took care of them). The derivative trades should have been margined but either weren't or the collateral used for margining was itself bad. The bigger counterparty wanted money to unwind the derivative and couldn't get it from the failed bank.

For example, in 2009 the FDIC took over a Bank that had entered into a 5 year interest rate swap with a notional amount of $100 million. The bank wanted to hedge a pool of newly originated fixed rate mortgages that it held on its balance sheet.

The risk was that rates increase and the fixed rate mortgages would decrease in value. To hedge that risk, the bank entered into a swap to pay a fixed rate to a counterparty and receive floating.

As interest rates declined during the financial crisis, the OTC derivative decreased in value. Paying 4% fixed to receive floating rate Libor when the market is pay 3 % fixed rate means a loss.

Unfortunately, the mortgage didn't increase in value due to credit and other factors. This points out the danger of partially hedging the risks of an asset. The asset can be subject to risks A (credit) and B (interest rates). You hedge B (interest rates) with a swap. A takes down the asset and B takes down the derivative. Both sides lose.

The FDIC derivative manager had to put "lipstick on the pig" and could not simply unwind the mortgage and pay off the loss on the derivative.

The strategy chosen was an "assignment". Most derivatives can be transferred to another counterparty with the other counterparties approval. The dealer would rather face another liquid dealer than a bankrupt small bank!

The task was to discover a solvent dealer that would accept assignment for the least cost since that new dealer was assuming a trade that was currently at a loss. The cost would be paid by the failed bank (ultimately the taxpayer) but the bank would be out of the swap at the least cost.

When the FDIC manager finished the assignment process, they paid money to a new dealer to take over their obligations to the original dealer .

Assignment allowed the swap to be liquid again!

18A3. Mortgage origination hedging

The business of mortgage banking, of course, is lending people money to buy a home. The lender quotes a rate to the borrower and sometime later (45 days?) the mortgage closes and the payments begin.

Instead of keeping the loan and getting the payments over time, the mortgage banker sells the loan typically to the Government National Mortgage Association (GNMA), the Federal National Mortgage Association (FNMA), or The Federal Home Loan Mortgage Association (Freddie Mac).

These agencies buy loans at market. Since it takes 45+ days to create the mortgage and the lender has locked in a rate over that period, the lender is at risk if rates go up. The (say) 5% mortgage is not worth $100 for every $100 par if rates go up even though it was worth $100 in the beginning of the period when the rate was quoted. If rates go up, the mortgage banker loses.

To counter that risk, the mortgage banker could short a TBA or buy an option on a mortgage TBA.

A TBA is a derivative on a pool of mortgages with a certain coupon but exact characteristics beyond that (for example, loan to value, credit score of borrower, etc.) are "To Be Announced". For the most part, they are derivatives on pools of newly originated mortgages that will settle (say) 1 month from now.

TBA's can be shorted. Thus, the derivative can pay you if prices drop. You can short the same coupon you quoted and it can be a TBA on the same agency as you plan to sell to (GNMA, FNMA, etc). Options also exist on them.

Shorting when the rate quote is made would be the answer except that the mortgage may not close in the 45 days. The borrower might have a credit issue not captured in the credit screen, the agency might change some small detail of what they accept, etc. Thus, closing is a risk – the other side of the hedge could go away and you are stuck "naked" in your short(s)!

The general answer is to short what you are sure will close and buy puts on the rest. The problem is cost. If your competitors don't hedge and you do, will you get any business?

To reduce this cost, it is tempting to sell calls on the mortgage. The premium you get is a partial hedge to rates going up but only a partial hedge. This is a good strategy in the current environment (late 2013) since the Fed has been buying securities and thus keeping rates low. The calls expire worthless and you keep the premium. However, if rates increase significantly, keeping the the call premium will not hedge the loss of worth on the mortgage.

18A4. Hedging short rates

Eurodollar futures are an excellent way to hedge the short term "CD" rates that a bank uses to have money to make longer term loans. The bank quotes (say) a three month rate and someone gives the bank money and earns that rate. The bank then usually loans that money out longer term. If they did nothing else and short rates went up, they might earn a negative spread over the life of the loan because the multiple short rates went up that are used to fund the longer loan.

To hedge this risk, the bank can short a Eurodollar future or series of Eurodollar futures (a "strip" of Eurodollar futures since they are shorted in future months sequentially). This is an example of liability hedging since the short term CD is a liability of the bank.

For example, the Federal Reserve Chairman suggested that short rates would remain artificially low through the beginning of 2015. Our bank treasurer is concerned about an increase in three month rates early in 2015. Assume the bank has a massive three month funding need exactly then. The treasurer would short March 2015 ED futures contracts to lock in the target yield. So if the price of the March ED futures contract is say 99.55 today, the implied forward 90 day ED futures yield is .45 basis points (100 - 99.55).

The "locked in" rate of 45bp assumes (a) the bank indeed issues debt in the future and (b) the zero spread of that debt doesn't change to 3 month Libor in the future. In the chart below, negative numbers means the bank pays and positive they receive. For example, -1.00 means the bank pays 1% for 3 months. The 3 month bank spread is assumed to be 0bp to 3 month Libor.

Borrowing Rate paid (Spot 3M Libor level)	Unwind future (Shorted @ .45)	All in "Cost"
(1.00)	.55	(.45)
(0.55)	.10	(.45)
(0.45)	.00	(.45)
(0.00)	(.45)	(.45)

Regardless of what rates do in the future, under the above two assumptions, the all-in borrowing rate (future and borrowing) is 45bp. This is because, in the top row of this example, All in borrowing = - Market Libor + (Market Libor − Futures rate) = -1 + (1-.45) = -.45. Market Libor is what you pay and defines futures unwind. All else cancels out.

How does one look at cost of hedging in this situation or indeed in any hedge? That depends on how one defines cost.

The best definition of cost is to equate risk of investments and compare return. If one chooses an alternative that has less return than the highest (and it has the same risk), cost is the difference in return. Said differently, all derivatives transform return and risk. Thus, cost must be measured comparing return across equivalent risk positions.

That contrasts with the typical textbook definition of cost as defined by "convergence". You locked in 45bp and if spot 3 month Libor was 20bp at the time, the cost would be defined as 25bp (45-20). However, comparing a hedged 45bp position with an unhedged 20bp position is apples and oranges. The two positions don't have the same risk. The correct approach is "would you rather have 45bp locked in or go unhedged and risk doing better or worse"? That clearly depends on one's return / risk tradeoff and perhaps defined in the "efficient frontier"- the best returns relative to different risks.

18B. Fixed Income Credit Derivatives

According to New York Insurance derivatives law (which many insurance companies comply with), insurance companies are allowed to use derivatives to hedge, "replicate", and do income generation.

Income generation means selling covered calls on owned securities. It is replication that requires some explanation.

The replication trade is very specific. One sells protection by doing a credit derivative trade (say, sells 5 year protection on IBM). One then finds a bond they own (say, 5 year Exxon) and "pairs" the two. That is, they are allowed to treat the two as one for reporting and reserving purposes by sending the two into the Insurance Security Valuation Office (SVO) in New York. Implicitly, the regulators are saying there is little difference between owning IBM corporate bonds and owning Exxon and selling a credit derivative on IBM.

The logic is strongest if one believes Exxon is "bulletproof" (will not default). In that case, if IBM defaults, sell Exxon and presumably one gets the money to close out the credit derivative. The money required is the par amount of credit derivative. This requires Exxon to always be par or above in market value.

If the above conditions held over the life of the trade, it would appear that one truly would replicate an IBM corporate bond. Person one buys IBM for (say) $100 par, it defaults and they get recovery. Person two buys Exxon for (say) $100, sells protection on IBM. IBM defaults, Person two sells Exxon, delivers the $100 and gets back IBM recovery.

Both people paid $100 in the beginning and got the recovery of IBM in the end upon default.

18C. The Other Value Drivers

18C1. Public Equity - Valuing Employee Stock Options

Black-Scholes is commonly used to value employee stock options when granted. However, there are many reasons this overstates the value. First, the employee typically loses all option value if they leave the company before vesting. Thus, one must measure the probability of staying from grant to vesting date and multiply that by the option price.

Second, consider the time between vesting and option expiration. If one leaves during this time, one only gets the difference between current stock price and option strike. One only gets "intrinsic" value and no "time" value. Said differently, an at the money option (current stock price = strike) with some time to expiration is worth something with regular options but the employee gets nothing if they exercise their options. The employee must exercise only at option expiration to realize the time value.

18C2. Private Equity – Bill Ackman and CP

Bill Ackman is a US "activist" hedge fund manager. He saw an opportunity in CP (the Canadian Pacific railway). He operated much like a private equity investor in this transaction. That is, he took over control of the company. He didn't have to borrow as is traditional in an LBO (Leveraged Buy Out). He used the funds in the hedge fund.

He had an interesting strategy. Hunter Harrison, the CEO of the successful railway Canadian National (CN), had recently retired from that railway. He was interested in being CEO of CP. The bet was his leadership skills would transfer. The stage was set.

What follows is an alleged timeline of events published on May 17, 2012 in Thestar, the online site of the Toronto Star newspaper.

In this discussion there is mention of a proxy vote. This means the shareholders would vote and decide the outcome.

Sept. 23, 2011 — Pershing Square Capital Management begins acquiring a stake in Canadian Pacific Railway, spending $1.4 billion, the largest single initial commitment to any investment for the U.S. hedge fund.

Oct. 28 — Pershing Square discloses in a filing with the Securities and Exchange Commission that it has acquired 12.2 per cent of outstanding shares, which later grew to 14.2 per cent. It noted it expected to engage in discussions over the future plans of the company.

Oct. 29 — CP's chairman John Cleghorn holds two telephone discussions with Pershing Square's Bill Ackman, who indicated he would be seeking significant change to the management team.

Nov. 2 — Ackman and two other Pershing Square officials meet in Montreal with Cleghorn and president and CEO Fred Green. Ackman says CP could get an operating ratio to 65 in four years, if former CN Rail executive Hunter Harrison took the helm.

Nov. 2 to 4 — CP's board of directors meets to discuss Pershing Square.

Nov. 4 — Further discussions between Cleghorn and Ackman, where he asks for a board spot for him and Paul Hilal, a Pershing Square partner.

Nov. 18 — Cleghorn advises Ackman that he will recommend the board meet with Ackman to consider his candidacy for board seat.

Nov. 21 — Board meets with CP's advisers. Board agrees to interview Ackman for board position, as well another candidate to boost railroad industry experience, but say they won't consider Hilal, who has no particular railroad expertise.

Dec. 11 — Ackman meets with governance committee in Calgary, and asks board to meet with Hilal.

Dec 12, 13 — Board holds meeting where Pershing Square's proposal is discussed.

Dec. 13 — Governance committee recommends that Ackman, Tony Ingram and Edmond Harris, both with railway backgrounds, be appointed to board. Pershing Square also discloses through regulatory filing its shares now total 14.2 per cent.

Dec. 14 — Cleghorn offers Ackman board seat, subject to confidentiality and standstill agreements.

Dec. 15 — Ingram and Harris are appointed to board.

Dec. 23 — Lawyer for Pershing Square says hedge fund will not sign confidentiality and standstill agreements.

Dec. 30 — News breaks that Pershing Square wants retired CN executive Hunter Harrison to be CP's next CEO.

Jan. 3 — On behalf of board, Cleghorn send open letter to Ackman, about inaccuracies in media reports, but says the board is willing to continue dialogue with Pershing Square

Jan. 4. — Ackman sends email to Cleghorn, with the subject line War and Peace, warning that "a border skirmish" would turn into "a nuclear winter" if his demands for two board seats and Harrison as CEO are not met. He warns that Pershing Square will initiate a proxy contest.

Jan. 9 — After board meeting the day before, CP issues an open letter to shareholders, saying the board is executing a clear plan to boost efficiency.

Jan. 13 — Canadian National Railway issues news release that states if Hunter Harrison takes a position with CP, it would violate a noncompete agreement.

Jan. 23 — CN begins legal action against Harrison in U.S. District Court in Illinois over possible breach of his agreements. Pershing Square said it will guarantee payments owed to Harrison.

CP also announces that it would hold annual meeting on May 17 in Calgary. Earlier that day, Pershing Square had sent CP a requisition for a special meeting, but withdrew after the annual meeting's announcement.

Jan. 24 — Pershing files document identifying five nominees to the board as well as the start of a proxy fight. In the months to come, it adds two other candidates.

Feb. 6 — Pershing holds a town hall at the Hilton hotel in Toronto, where Ackman as well as the other board nominees are presented to shareholders, analysts and the media. Hunter Harrison is also present, who says he is eager to come out of retirement. He also says he has bought $5 million worth of shares to show his interest in the job.

Feb. 10 — CN amends its lawsuit against Harrison, and cancels his pension and other payments due to him, worth $40 million. CN also advises that it would consider filing an injunction to block Harrison from going to CP.

March 27 — At an investor day in Toronto, top CP officials meet with analysts and media for first time, warning if shareholders side with Pershing, it would be risky and lead to uncertainty and possible dysfunction.

April 20 — CP reports strong first-quarter earnings, hitting a record $142-million profit, which officials say shows the company is on the right track. Pershing isn't swayed, saying good weather helped boost results. Ackman also says its five nominees, not Pershing candidates, have all bought CP shares totalling about $2 million.

April 23 — CP announces it is boosting its next quarterly dividend, payable on July 30, to 35 cents a share, up from 30 cents.

May 2 — Despite media suggestions that CP is prepared to reach a settlement with Pershing Square, by granting four board seats as long as Harrison does not become president and CEO, both sides insist there is no deal, and no talks are under way.

May 3 — Proxy advisory firm ISS recommends Ackman's slate and withholding votes against certain CP directors including Cleghorn and Green.

May 7 — Ontario Teachers' Pension Plans says it will back Ackman's slate.

May 8 — Ackman speaks at Bloomberg's economic summit in Toronto where he says he won't make a deal because shareholders deserve a vote. He says of 36 per cent of proxies cast, include ones he controls, Pershing's slate has won more than 95 per cent.

May 9 — Proxy advisory firm Glass Lewis & Co also backs Pershing's slate.

May 17 — CP announces Fred Green has resigned as CEO and President of the company. The company also announced six directors, including Green, would not be standing for re-election.

We fast forward a year – Alleged events posted in Business in Canada (BIC), June 4, 2013

Ackman's journey with Canadian Pacific has been fraught with drama. When he declared his stake on October 28, 2011, the railroad company was down 4.5 percent year-to-date. A furious battle with the firm's management soon erupted. After a leak revealed Ackman's displeasure with CEO Fred Green and his pick to replace him – which was rejected by the board – the activist investor struck back with a vengeance. He threatened (and went on to declare) war in the form of a proxy contest, as shown in this alleged email excerpt to company Chairman John Cleghorn:

Based on yesterday and my not receiving a return call from you, the probability of war occurring has gone up meaningfully. War is not my preference and it has been extremely rare for us. We have had only two proxy contests in 25 or so active engagements with public companies in the last eight years.

No stranger to spectacle, Ackman presented his case to shareholders at the Toronto Hilton in early February 2012, an event at which Hunter Harrison <u>also addressed the crowd</u>.

On May 17, 2012, the management of Canadian Pacific chose to hold up the white flag rather than wait a few hours for a proxy battle to seal its fate. CEO Fred Green <u>resigned,</u> while Cleghorn and other directors announced they would leave the board. Ackman's handpicked candidate, Hunter Harrison, was then installed as CEO.

The numbers don't lie: this has been a spectacular investment. As of Monday's close, shares of Canadian Pacific were up 112.38 percent (TSX) and 104.23 percent (NYSE) from the date Pershing Square declared its stake. Here's a chart that shows the stock's performance and some milestones in the Ackman saga:

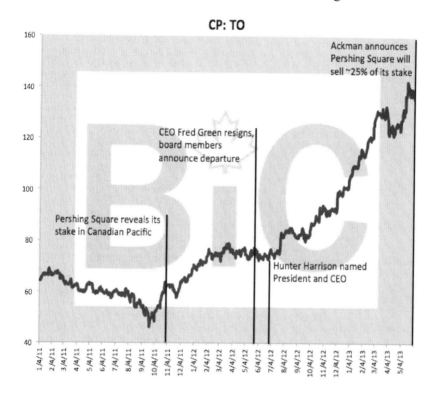

18C3. Commodity - Silver – alleged events posted on http://www.traderslog.com/hunt-brothers-silver/

In the early seventies, amidst political upheaval, inflationary pressures and stagnant economic growth, the richest family in America (at the time), the Hunt family of Texas, tried to corner the market on precious metals. As a way to hedge themselves from the rampart printing of dollars the US government was doing, the Hunts decided to accumulate large amounts of hard asset investments. Since gold could not be held by private citizens back then, the Hunt brothers focused on silver.

In 1979, the Hunt brothers, along with a group of wealthy Arabs, formed a pool buying silver and silver futures. The Hunt brothers used their positions in silver futures to acquire more of the physical metal. As cash was continually losing value due to inflation, the Hunts decided to settle their long silver futures contracts with delivery of silver, instead of cash settlement. Before too long, they had amassed over 200 million ounces of silver which was about half of the world's supply.

Prices soon started to appreciate. When they started, the price of silver was below $5 ounce. By late 1979/early 1980 prices had increased tenfold and were trading near $55/oz. During this rise in prices, the COMEX and Chicago Board of Trade (CBOT) only had about 120 million ounces of silver between them. As prices went higher and new buyers got into the market, the exchanges became increasingly fearful of defaulting. As the Hunts owned 77% of the world's silver, either in physical form or futures contracts, the market had been cornered.

Things began to change once Paul Volker was named Chairman of the Federal Reserve. Volker was determined to get inflation under control by raising interest rates. Couple that with changes in trading rules at the CBOT and COMEX, prices soon plummeted. Things had gotten so out of whack that COMEX only accepted liquidation orders, effectively halting silver from going higher. The CBOT set limits on the amount of silver any one entity could hold and raised margins. Not surprisingly prices came down significantly quickly and were trading near $10 by the end of March 1980.

The precipitous drop in prices meant huge losses for many speculators and ultimately forced the Hunt brothers into bankruptcy. By the mid-80s, the Hunt brothers had more than a billion dollars in liabilities they could not meet. At their peak, the

Hunt brothers had held over $4.5 billion in silver on their $1 billon investment. On March 25, 1980, the Hunt brothers couldn't meet their $135 million margin call, forcing the Hunt brothers to 'shut it down.' In August of 1988, the Hunts were convicted of conspiring to manipulate the market.

It was in late March 1980 that we had "Silver Thursday", a day where the price of silver went from roughly $20/oz to $10/oz, a loss of over 50%. Ultimately, the Hunts had to be bailed out by New York banks so they could make good on their obligations. Their obligations had grown so large that the government forced the banks to issue credit so that wide spread failures could be prevented.

The Hunts had exposed themselves to huge amounts of leverage, which worked great in the beginning. It was this leverage from the futures markets that ultimately did them in. The Hunts ended up losing because they couldn't fight the Fed and the system as a whole. The exchanges changed the rules once they saw they were out maneuvered and couldn't default, which would have led to widespread failures. Not only that, but many of the regulators who helped change the rules were also short silver.

In the end, cornering a market is not only illegal but immoral as well. In a truly free market, cornering a market wouldn't work as alternative investments would gain favor. Also, as supply is taken off the market, buying the last bit of any commodity would become prohibitively expensive. If the Hunts had only bought physical silver, there was nothing that financial industry or the government could have done. Conversely, if they only bought physical silver, the market probably wouldn't have gone up that much, but they never would have had any futures contracts obligations to meet. Today, the price of silver is finally close to testing the artificial highs of the early 80s. Similar to the late 70s, inflation is spreading, political situations around the globe are precarious at best and energy prices are near highs. Position limits and daily marked to the market accounting, makes it nearly impossible to corner any market today. In the end, the Hunts tried to fight financial industry insiders and the US government, only to have the rules of the game changed in the middle of the game. But don't feel too bad for them, although they lost huge amounts of money, they still are worth several hundreds of millions of dollars, each.

18C4. Currency – Alleged events about Soros and shorting the British Pound in 1992.

Alleged events written by "KIRKUK" and posted on

http://answers.yahoo.com/question/index?qid=20130404232443 AA8NmKK

In 1990, Great Britain joined the EMS and the rate of the pound (GBP) was fixed at the level of 2,95 (DEM) with a permissible currency corridor ± 6%. By the middle of the 1992 thanks to the ERM, a considerable decrease of the inflation tempo in European countries- members of the EMS, was reached. Nevertheless, the artificial maintenance of the currency rates in the limits of the currency corridor arose doubts of the investors. The situation got worse after the reunion of West and East Germany in 1989. The weakness of West Germany's economy brought to the incensement of the national outlay, which forced Bundesbank to issue more money. This policy brought to inflation, and Bundesbank reacted to this by uprising the interest rate. The high interest rates attracted foreign investors, this, in its turn, caused an excess demand on the Deutschemark, and resulted in the growth of its rates. The Great Britain, being bound by the EMS agreement, was to maintain its national currency rates within the fixed limits of the currency corridor versus the Deutschemark. The British economy at that time was destabilized; the unemployment rate of the country was high. The uprising of the interest rate after Germany in such conditions could only make the situation worse. But there were no other possibilities to strengthen the domestic currency rate in the near term. At that time, George Soros and many other investors considered, that the GB would not be able to maintain the domestic currency rate at the needed level, and it would have either to announce about its devaluation, or refrain from the ERM. George Soros took a decision to contract debts for the pounds (GBP), and to sell them for the Deutschemarks (DEM), and invest them in the German assets. As a result, almost GBP 10 billion was sold. George Soros was not alone thinking in this direction, and many investors followed his actions. As a consequence of such speculations, the unstable economical situation in Britain became even worse. The Bank of England in the attempt to set the situation right and to increase the currency rate repurchased for its reserves around GBP 15 billion. But it did not bring the desired result. Then, on the 16th of September 1992, on the day, which would further be called "Black Wednesday", the Bank of England declared about the interest rate increase from 10% to 12% in the attempt to neutralize the boom, but the expectations of the English politicians did not prove. The investors, who sold pounds, were sure that they would gain an enormous profit after the further downfall of its rate. A few hours later the Bank of England claimed to increase the interest rate to 15%, but the traders kept selling pounds in large quantities. This continued till 19:00 of that very day, later on the Chief Secretary to the Treasury Norman Lamont pronounced, that the Great Britain was seceding the European Exchange Rate Mechanism (ERM) and the interest rate would be lowered to 10%. From that day on, the pound rate fall had started, which fell by 15% versus the Deutschemark and by 25% versus the US dollar within 5 weeks. This brought a gigantic profit to the Quantum Fund – within only one month George Soros gained around 2 billion US dollars, buying for the German assets the significantly cheaper pounds. The down falling of the pound currency rate versus the US dollar after the above described events is shown on the image. As it can be noticed, that only in September 1992 the pound fell by almost 3000   ticks!

Thus, George Soros, "the man who broke the Bank of England" showed, to what extent the Central Banks can be vulnerable to currency speculations of the large investors in the conditions of the artificially maintained currency rates. The use of the borrowed funds allowed George Soros to gather wealth within just a few weeks, which set a beginning to his charity work. As we have seen it, in order to prevent the negative influence of the currency speculations on the economy of the country, Central Banks create reserves in the form of foreign assets. But as the practice has shown, such reserves can prove to be ineffective, if they are opposed to the large capitals of the investors, who have the same goal.

Today, the currency market Forex is far more liquid than at the beginning of the 90's Therefore, no investor, even having a billion capital, will hardly be able to influence on the currency rate for a long time. "Black Wednesday" of September, 1992 is left far behind, but the historic facts should not be ignored, because the history has a tendency to recur.

18C5. Real Estate

The most recent financial collapse (of 2008) arguably started with credit derivatives on subprime mortgages. Not surprisingly, these are mortgages issued to below prime borrowers. It has been said there was little documentation supporting the possibility of repayment. It has been said the main argument for repayment was "home prices always go up, don't they"? Thus, if the borrower doesn't repay, repossess the home.

So, the loan was made, the original lender sold the loan into the pool of a structured investment. Investors bought tranches. The original lender was out and had no risk.

A wrinkle to this story is well documented. AIG sold protection on senior tranches created from these subprime mortgages. The credit derivative was on a senior tranche. They are an insurance company and as stated previously, insurance companies can only hedge, replicate and do income generation trades according to New York Insurance Law. This is not any of those trades.

They did the trades in the holding company since technically that is not an insurance company. It owns an insurance company but is not itself an insurance company.

So, earnings looked good because of the credit derivative premium AIG got. The problem was they did very many trades and didn't reserve for the potential loss if default. The credit derivatives started to be marked against AIG as the real estate market worsened. AIG did not have the liquidity to meet the margin calls.

Who was the beneficial owner of protection on these tranches? It is well documented that several large hedge fund clients of major brokerage houses bought the protection.

What follows is alleged events from High Beam Research by Rodney Ruff

http://www.highbeam.com/topics/american-international-group-aig-subprime-mortgage-crisis-t10020

Overview

New York-based American International Group (AIG) was one of a number of companies, along with Bear Stearns and Lehman Brothers, hit by the subprime mortgage crisis of September 2008. Founded in 1919 as American Asiatic Underwriters, AIG had grown into a multinational corporation doing business in 130 countries in such diverse businesses as aircraft leasing and life insurance, along with its principal business of mortgage insurance. In early 2007, AIG reported assets of $1 trillion, with $110 billion in income. It did business in 130 countries, with 116,000 employees servicing 74 million customers. Its stock was one of the 10 most widely held stocks in 401(k) portfolios.

However, since 1987, AIG, through its AIG Financial Products division, had been involved in credit default swaps (insurance contracts covering securities against losses incurred by defaulting on payments), which by 2008 had reached an estimated total of $450 billion. Also, it had contracted its securities management to companies such as ICP Asset Management and Moore Capital, which sought to make money for AIG through lending stocks and bonds owned by its life insurance subsidiaries to banks and hedge funds. The money generated from lending these securities was mostly invested in residential-mortgage-backed securities. When the value of such securities plummeted in 2008, AIG was hit hard.

with credit default swaps creating a $14.7 billion share of its overall reported loss in the second quarter of $26.2 billion and another $16.5 billion in collateral on its credit default swap portfolio.

The Bailout

The staggering losses prompted Moody's to threaten to lower AIG's credit ratings if it could not raise sufficient capital to meet the capital reserve requirements for the "AAA" rating AIG had held to that point. AIG's chief executive officer, Robert B. Willumstad, met with senior executives and bankers from the Blackstone Group, Citigroup and JPMorgan Chase, planning to raise capital and sell assets to meet Moody's requirements.

Unfortunately, the collapse of Lehman Brothers torpedoed those plans, forcing AIG to appeal to New York State insurance regulators for permission to borrow $20 billion from its subsidiaries. Although approval was granted, that amount was soon determined to be insufficient. When AIG contacted officials of the Federal Reserve Board to notify them of its situation, the necessary amount had become $30 billion. However, by the time Treasury Secretary Henry Paulson Jr. met with AIG executives on September 13, a subsequent audit of AIG's books raised the necessary amount to $40 billion, an amount raised after yet another audit by JPMorgan Chase to $65 billion.

With the threat of a government takeover looming, prospective investors backed out. A Monday morning attempt by the Fed on September 15 to line up $75 billion in bank loans failed, at which point both Moody's and Standard and Poor's lowered AIG's credit rating to ?A,? raising the amount of collateral AIG would need to produce to cover its credit default swap contracts to nearly $100 billion.

Paulson notified President George W. Bush about the situation, while aides contacted congressional leaders to arrange a briefing with leaders of both parties in both houses. Paulson and Fed Chairman Benjamin Bernanke laid out a plan to loan AIG $85 billion in exchange for 79.9 percent ownership of the company.

The actual loan would be through the Federal Reserve Bank of New York, then headed by Timothy Geithner, Paulson's eventual successor as treasury secretary. Several weeks later, on October 7, the Fed pledged another $37.8 billion in loans after AIG paid $18.7 billion on its credit default swaps.

On November 10, after disclosing that it had posted $37.3 billion on the swaps, AIG received a reduced interest rate and three years to pay back its loan from the government, which had become part of a $150 billion rescue package consisting of a $60 billion loan, $50 billion to buy mortgage-linked assets, and another $40 billion in capital investments.

Restructuring and Results

The bailout permitted AIG to continue to operate, but not as it had before. Its American Life Insurance Company (ALICO) and Delaware American Life Insurance Company (DelAm) subsidiaries were sold to MetLife in 2010, taking AIG out of the international life insurance business. (The ALICO sale earned AIG $16.8 billion.) A deal to sell its American International Assurance Group (AIA) to Prudential Financial that year for $35.5 billion fell through because Prudential shareholders would not underwrite the price. Instead, AIG took AIA public on the Hong Kong Stock Exchange in October of that year, generating another $20 billion. However, AIG did sell its Star Life Insurance and Edison Life Insurance to Prudential in February 2011 for $4.8 billion, after selling Nan Shan Life the previous month to Ruen Chen of Taiwan for $2.16 billion.

Sales of these subsidiaries enabled AIG to post earnings for the fourth quarter of 2010 of $11.2 billion, offsetting its losses in the first three quarters, and providing a sharp contrast to the $8.87 billion loss of the fourth quarter of the previous year. Overall earnings for 2010 were $7.8 billion, in contrast to the overall $10.9 billion loss in 2009.

In April 2011, AIG announced plans to sue ICP Asset Management and Moore Capital for losses suffered insuring ICP's mortgage securities. The suit asks for $350 million in damages from ICP, as well as the profits made by Moore. AIG also plans to sue banks such as Bank of America and Goldman Sachs that created the over $40 million in mortgage bonds it had purchased from them.

18D. Tax considerations

Tax issues are also a part of trading. Currently, corporations are taxed the same for capital gains and income but gains and losses don't transfer across the two. So, care is spent making sure the two baskets fill up evenly.

18E. Accounting

Earnings (on the income statement) are more important than surplus (on the balance sheet). Anything that causes earnings to fluctuate is taboo.

Derivatives are marked through earnings in GAAP accounting. Thus hedging with derivatives (where the change in derivatives in price and the change in the hedged security both go through earnings) is preferable to an outright derivative position that gets marked through earnings with no offset.

But what about a structured note? It can contain derivatives and be marked through surplus under certain circumstances! For example, a "tranche" referencing a pool of credit derivatives is marked through surplus. A structured note that has an equity derivative embedded into a corporate issuance is currently split. The note fluctuations in mark to market go through surplus but the equity derivative marks go through the income statement! The structured note is bifurcated!

18F. Industry specific applications

18F1. Securities Brokerage.

You are a broker suggesting investments to individuals and corporations. How do you use the information in this book?

Individuals typically have a large amount of equities in their portfolios. Selling calls on the equities is one way to start. If the individual believes the stock is worth holding on to but believes it will "rest" in price for awhile, sell calls and collect premium.

Another approach is to realize futures or forwards are an alternative to margined trades. Instead of borrowing on margin and buying, go long the future if the financing rate is lower than interest paid on margin. You will be long forward at a lower level than the margined trade since forwards are lower with smaller financing rates.

Of course, hedge funds and other spot settling funded investments should be added assuming they look well from a risk/return perspective.

Finally, structured assets can add protection as compared to investments in a portfolio of the same assets in the structured pool. This is because structured assets have equity tranches. That is, if only some of the pool defaults, you are better off with structure as long as the default doesn't "eat into" your tranche.

The tradeoff is severity risk. For example, if you own a tranche that starts to default after 10% of the pool is gone, the next 15% could wipe you out if that is the "width" of your tranche. Your $100 investing in the tranche is all gone if 25% defaults but only $25 of your $100 is gone if you invest in the pool.

18F2. Hedge Fund

This group is probably the broadest user of alternatives.

One of the most used trades is arbitrage. For example, suppose the future is a higher price than carry and delivery option calculations suggest. Hedge funds do a "basis trade" – they borrow and buy the cash and sell the future.

One of the earliest arbitrage credit derivative trades involved buying a bond and buying protection. If the bond experienced default concerns, the future would move more in spread than the "cash" bond and the gain on the credit derivative was greater than the loss on the bond. If nothing happened, the carry on the bond earned was often greater than the credit derivative premium. One was paid to possibly have a profit!

Chapter 19. Setting up Alternative Programs in Different Businesses (Tests needed, Suggested Procedures, etc.)

What is the work environment associated with someone who wants to pursue a career in alternatives?

19A. Corporate Environment

There are two programs implied by the material in this book in the corporate environment - first, an outright derivative trading program and second, an alternatives program.

19A1. Derivative Trading Program

Derivatives are "on something". In a large corporate environment, someone is managing that "something". For example, someone is already managing corporate bonds but there are also derivatives on corporate bonds. If the derivative person is a separate person, the two might disagree and one buys what the other sells. The only workable solution the author has found is to have the derivative person act as a consultant to the person trading the underlying security. The two are a team, sharing compensation and trading in unison.

There are many underlying assets that derivatives reference. Thus, ideally, the derivatives desk is in partnership with many people trading the underlying assets.

Perhaps the most important rule for the derivative person (and securities person) is to never have the same person trade and settle the trade. There is too much temptation to "hide" mistakes.

Once the trade is done, the issue is marking an OTC derivative trade. A system is needed that records the trade AND subsequently marks the trade. One example system is Bloomberg. The marks could be done monthly and checked with broker marks quarterly. Of course, if Dodd-Frank functions as anticipated, OTC trades should have more transparency since they will be like exchange trades – prices should be posted on an electronic exchange.

Some corporations have adopted approval of derivative "programs". This requires a write-up of the proposed trade and the legal, regulatory, accounting, tax and credit implications. The maximum size is also stated. The investment committee approves the "program".

This allows freedom to execute when market conditions are appropriate. It is not cumbersome if the program is defined somewhat broadly. For example, requesting using credit derivatives paired with bonds instead of buying the bond the credit derivative is on (see prior chapter for an example). Many different credit derivative markets could be paired with many different bonds.

19A2. Alternatives Program

The Chapter outlining Alternatives suggests many different investments. Where should one start?

Perhaps the easiest place is hedge funds. After all, they are supposed to be hedged. If appropriate (for example, a long-short stock hedge fund), it is suggested you compare the fund to mixtures of traditional assets. After all, the fund is hedged and that means it should be compared to a diversified traditional asset mixture since diversification is the main means of risk reduction in traditional programs.

For example, does the hedge fund you are considering outperform a balanced fund of (say) 60% stocks, 30% bonds and 10% cash? In other words, don't compare a hedge fund to just one traditional asset. By definition, certainly a long-short hedge fund is a blend of traditional assets – so compare a particular fund to a blend.

After (perhaps) long-short hedge funds, a credit fund might be next. Here the hedge is buying for 20 cents on the dollar something you believe will be 50 cents or more later. Obviously, this is best done opportunistically. An event needs to happen.

Perhaps next is mezzanine funds. Corporations run on bonds. Mezzanine funds are very similar to "regular" bonds but have the potential for more yield due to being in a different part of the capital structure (basically subordinated to investment grade bonds). If default occurs, they are paid after "senior" debt obligations.

Currency might be next, followed by commodities.

19B. Securities Brokerage and RIAs

In this environment, know your customer is the rule.

A traditional broker takes a securities test (Series 7) from NASD (National Association of Securities Dealers). Typically, traditional assets are bought and sold but options might be used. The most common options strategy is covered call writing. You own a stock and sell a call if you think the stock is going to "pause" in price appreciation.

A new entry into this field is a Registered Investment Advisor Representative or Firm. This designation has increased significantly in numbers since the late 1990s to 2014.

An RIA differs from the traditional broker. Traditional brokers are usually compensated by number of trades done for a client. This might lead to "over trading the account" ("churning" the account). In contrast, an RIA is paid based on a percentage of assets under management. Thus, the value of the account must increase for them to be paid more. This should align their interests with the client interests.

These firms can be registered with the Securities Exchange Commission (SEC) but must maintain a minimum of $90 million in assets under management (AUM) to remain regulated by them. Smaller advisors are regulated by the Attorney General in the advisor's state where their main office is located.

The rules for regulation, regardless of the advisor's AUM, are based on the 1940 Act. All advisors must take a Series 65 exam or a Series 7 and Series 66 exam to practice as a RIA. A website for further information is www.FINRA.org.

It should be noted there are a lot of mergers in this area. This is because of the expense of compliance due to the large number of rules that have come out because of the financial crisis of 2008.

19C. Hedge Fund

In this environment, snow your customer is the rule. Just kidding.

The different types of hedge funds have been covered. Choosing a fund to join is mainly a matter of chemistry with the current employees and your interest.

19D. Private Equity

In this environment, play golf with your customer is the rule. Just kidding again.

These transactions are complex and thus require a broad range of expertise. This means it is best, certainly in the beginning, to join a large firm (if possible).

APPENDICES

A. Funded Alternative Security Matrix - Cash is needed on settlement

Major Value Driver	Unstructured	Structured
Interest Rates	1	8
Credit	2	9
Equity	3	10
Commodity	4	11
Currency	5	12
Real Estate	6	13
Other	7	14

Examples of Investments belonging to the cells in the matrix. These examples are looked at from the perspective of the investor, not what the entity itself invests in.

Unstructured

1. Hedge and Mezzanine Funds
2. Hedge Funds
3. Hedge Funds, Private Equity
4. Hedge Funds
5. Hedge Funds, Spot Currency Exchange, and Gold and Silver Coins
6. Hedge Funds, Real Estate Whole Loans
7. Infrastructure Funds, Mineral rights

Structured

8. CBO, CLO tranches
9. CDO tranches, Convertible bonds
10. Private Equity, Convertible bonds, ETF's
11.
12. First to default baskets
13. Tranches of CMO's (Residential), and CMBS (Commercial)
14.

B. Unfunded Alternative Security Matrix - Position needs minimal cash at settlement.

Major Value Driver	OTC Forwards	Options	Exchange Futures	Options	Notional on Dec/2012 OTC	Exchange
Interest Rates	1	8	15	22	489.7	22.6
Credit	2	9	16	23	25.1	
Equity	3	10	17	24	6.3	1.2
Commodity	4	11	18	25	0.5	
Currency	5	12	19	26	67.8	0.2
Real Estate	6	13	20	27	589.4	24.0
Other	7	14	21	28		

Forwards and Futures can be spot starting or deferred. Options are on the forwards. Each cell
can be structured or unstructured (a typical option). Notional sizes in trillions from WWW.BIS.Org.

Unstructured
1. Notes and Bonds, Libor Swaps, Repo's and Reverse's
2. Single Name Credit Derivatives
3. Active forward market on single "names"
4. Active forward market on single assets
5. Active forward market on single assets
6. Most RE buys 45-90 days forward
7.
8. Very active options market
9.
10. Very active options market
11. Very active options market
12. Very active options market

Structured
1. Total Return Bond Swaps, TBA's
2. Index Credit Derivatives
3. S&P Total Return Swaps
4. Commodity Basket Swaps
5. Currency Basket Swaps
6. CMBX
7.
8.
9.
10. S&P 500 options are very active
11.
12.

(Continued on next page)

Appendix to Chapter 2, Cont'd

Unstructured	Structured
13.	13.
14	14.
15. Note, Bond and Libor futures are active	15.
16.	16.
17. Equity futures very active	17.
18.	18.
19. Trade on Philadelphia exchange	19.
20.	20.
21.	21.
22. Active options markets	22.
23.	23.
24. Active options markets	24.
25.	25.
26.	26.
27.	27.
28.	28.

1. Assume a 15M deal is financed by a capital structure of 40% equity, 60% debt.
   The two investors are the fund and the General Partners (GPs) in the fund.
   The two investors own the following at the beginning.

Type of Asset	Additional Asset Information	Asset Owner	% of Total Deal	Interest Rate	Term	Order of Payment at Deal Maturity
Debt	High Yield Bonds	Fund	60%	8%	10 Years	1
Equity	Pref Shares	Fund	30%	10%	N/A	2
Equity	Common	Fund	8%	Dividends	N/A	3
Equity	Common	GP	2%	Dividends	N/A	4

2. Assume, during the deal, the interim cashflows pay the dividends, pay the high
   yield coupons and partially amortize the high yield bond principal to 3.5 million.

3. Assume the deal is sold in 7 years for 17 million. What do each of the parties get?

Type of Asset	Additional Asset Information	Asset Owner	% of Total Deal	Beginning Investment $ $15,000,000	Ending Sale $ Distribution $17,000,000	IRR
Debt	High Yield Bonds	Fund	60%	$9,000,000	$3,500,000	8%
Equity	Pref Shares	Fund	30%	$4,500,000	$8,769,227	10%
Equity	Common	Fund	8%	$1,200,000	$3,784,618	18%
Equity	Common	GP	2%	$300,000	$946,155	18%

Calculating Discount Factors, Term Structure, Forward yields and other yield types

1. We start with a par curve. This is the yield at each maturity of typically the latest issue of of bonds (since they have a close to market price of $1 for every $1 "par" one gets at maturity). That is, the bond yield comes from coupon, not price appreciation.

2. From the par curve, we get discount factors for cash flows occurring at different times. These numbers, when multiplied by the future cashflows, bring the future values back to today. The set of discount factors for the different times is called term structure. Below we assume coupons (C1, C2, ...) are paid every 6 months (but quoted annually).

Periods (each 6 months)

1	2	3	4	5	6

C1	C2	C3	C4	C5	C6
1.5	2	2.5	3	3.5	4

df(1)	df(2)	df(3)	df(4)	df(5)	df(6)
0.992556	0.980272	0.963298	0.941831	0.916104	0.886391

Since they are par bonds, they are worth $1 today and mature at par (also $1). So:

For df(1) we have $1=(1.5/200)*df(1) + 1*df(1)$ OR,
for the 6 month discount factor, we have $df(1) = 1 / (1 + (C1 / 200))$

Consider df(2) We have $1=(2/200)*df(1) + (2/200)*df(2) + 1*df(2)$ OR,
for one year, $df(2)=(1-(C2/200)*df(1))/(C2/200 +1)$

Consider df(3) We have $1=(2.5/200)*df(1) + (2.5/200)*df(2) + (2.5/200)*df(3) + 1*df(3)$
So 1.5 year is $df(3)=(1-((C3/200)*(df(1)+df(2))))/(C3/200 + 1)$

3. Semi Annual Bond Equivalent Forward Yields (BEY Forwards)
Note: PV = FV * df. Since PV = 1 (par bonds), 1 / df = FV.

IN	FV of $1 today	
1	1.007500	=1/df(1)
2	1.020125	=1/df(2)
3	1.038100	=1/df(3)
4	1.061762	=1/df(4)
5	1.091579	=1/df(5)
6	1.128170	=1/df(6)

Our money in 5 years is our money after 2 years grown at the forward yield for 3 years.
We have $FV5 = FV2 * (1 + 2F3/200)^3$

This means in 2 for 3 (or 2F3) = $((FV5/FV2)^{(1/3)} - 1) * 200$
$2F3 = ((1.091579/1.020125)^{(1/3)} - 1) * 200$

2F3 =	4.564642	See the bold cell below

IN	FOR >>>> 1	2	3	4	5
1	2.506266	3.014493	3.527940	4.048095	4.576583
2	3.523996	4.040709	**4.564642**	5.097461	
3	4.558734	5.086959	5.624648		
4	5.616548	6.159686			
5	6.704258				
6					

4. All these rates are BEY. Other types of rates are below. Here F = Face = Par = FV

    a. Discount (dy)

        dy= ((F-P) / F) * (360 / t) where t is in days
        dy = 10% = (100-90)/100
        P=F * (1 - dy * t / 360)

    b. Money Market
       (Sometimes called
       Add On Yield)

        AOY= ((F-P)/P) * (360 / t)
        P=F / (1 + AOY * t / 360)

    c. bey (bond equivalent yield)

        P = F/ [(1+bey/2)^(2*t)] where t= number of years

    d. Continuous r

        P=F / e ^ (r*t) or P=F * e ^ (-r*t)

F=	100
r (.1=10%)=	0.1
t=	1
P=	90.4837

Since e^(r*t) = (1+bey/2)^(2*t)   r=   ln[(1+bey/2)^(2t)] / t
Thus, e^[(r*t)/(2*t)] = (1+bey/2)   bey=   ((e^ (r/2)) -1) * 2
                                  bey=   0.1025
That is, a 10% continuous yield is a 10.25% bey yield. Proof:

F = $1 * e ^ (r*t).	FV
For r = 10% & t = 1 year, FV=	1.105171

F = (1+bey/2)^(2*t)	FV
For bey = 10.25% & t = 1 year, FV=	1.105171

Appendix to Chapter 9 - Section A4

Other techniques for calculating discount factors

1. Multiple regression

Consider a matrix of securities as rows and the associated cash flows of coupon and par as columns. For example, let MP1 = the market price of security 1, MP2 = the market price as security 2, etc.

Months	0-6	6-12	12-18	18-24	24-30
Market price today					
MP1 = 100.1	$1	$1	$100	0	0
MP2 = 99.5	$1.5	$1.5	$1.5	$100	0
MP3 = 97.8	$2	$2	$2	$2	$2
Coefficients >>>	C1	C2	C3	C4	C5

Multiple Regression solves for the coefficients (C1, C2, ...) to create fitted prices. The Fitted Prices are the sum of the coefficients times the cash flows. For example

Fitted Price
FP1 = C1 * $ 1   + C2 * $ 1   + C3 * $ 100 + C4 * $ 0   + C5 * $ 0
FP2 = C1 * $ 1.5   + C2 * $ 1.5 + C3 * $ 1.5   + C4 * $ 100   + C5 * $ 0
FP3 = C1 * $ 2   + C2 * $ 2   + C3 * $ 2   + C4 * $ 2   + C5 * $ 2

Multiple Regression solves for the C1 - C5 such that the fitted prices are close to the market prices. It solves for the C1 - C5 such that the sum of $(MP1 - FP1)^2 +$ ....$+(MP3 - FP3)^2$ is minimal.

Notice that each time period has only one coefficient across securities.
This is a value similar to the discount factors calculated in 9A5.
Similar in that the coefficients multiply future values to get present values.
Different in that all securities influence the coefficients.

2. Interpolation techniques (A note)

It is difficult to find a set of securities that have cash flows with exact date matches. Ideally, this is required in all approaches that calculate term structure. It is tempting to think the solution is to shrink the time "buckets". The problem is then there are much fewer cash flows in a given "bucket".

Various interpolation techniques exist to adjust the timing of the cash flows so that there are decent samples in a time bucket.

~ 153 ~

Appendix to Chapter 9 - Sections A7a & A7b

Macaulay Duration as a measure of price sensitivity -
It is the percentage price change for a given percentage rate change

Price plus accrued interest is the present value of future flows (C(i)).

$PV(0)$ = sum(i=1 to N) of { $C(i) / (1+r)^i$ }
Where PV(0) is todays price plus accrued

$dPV(0) / dr$ = sum(i=1 to N) of { [-C(i) * i * (1+r) ^ (i-1)] / [(1+r)^(2i)] }
= (1/(1+r)) * sum(i=1 to N) of { [-C(i) * i] / [(1+r)^i] }
= - sum(i=1 to N) of { [PV(i) * i] / [1+r] }

This gives us a measure of price sensitivity (change in price or dPV(0)) for a change in rates (dr). However, Macaulay duration is the **percentage** change in price for a **percentage** change in rates. Thus, we have to multiply above by (1+r) / PV(0).

Finally, Macaulay duration = t = (dPV(0) / PV(0)) / (dr / (1+r))

For example

t=12 (12 six month periods or 6 years),   PV(0) = $124.234
1+r = 1.01, dr = .0001   (a basis point in yield)

dPV(0) = t * PV(0) * dr /(1+r)=$0.1476   Equation 1

Thus, $100 par bond, priced at $124.234 moves $0.1476
with a basis point movement (.0001) in yield if the duration is 6 years.

Appendix to Chapter 9 - Sections A7a & A7b, Cont'd

Macaulay Duration as a measure of time to minimum risk

The value of an investment in the future, V(T), is the value of the reinvested coupons and the price at T. Let these cashflows be C(i).

$$V(T) = \text{sum}(i{=}1 \text{ to } N) \text{ of } \{ C(i) * (1+r)^{\wedge}(T-i) \} \qquad 0{<}T{<}N \quad \text{Equation 2}$$

For example, assume N is 3 and coupons are paid every 6 months..

$$V(1) = C(1) + C(2)/(1+r) + C(3)/((1+r)^{\wedge}2) \qquad \text{T=1 and N=3}$$
$$V(2) = C(1) * (1+r) + C(2) + C(3)/(1+r) \qquad \text{T=2 and N=3}$$
$$V(3) = C(1)*(1+r)^{\wedge}2 + C(2)*(1+r) + C(3) \qquad \text{T=3 and N=3}$$

If T=1, we have just received the first coupon and the price is the sum of the other two terms. If T=2, we have received the first coupon, reinvested it for one period, received the second coupon and the price is the third term. If T=3, our worth is reinvested coupons and the final cash flow.

Assuming T=1, if rates go up, our worth goes down. If T=3, if rates go up, our worth goes up. Somewhere there is a balancing and we don't care if rates go up or down. We are "immunized" to rate movement.

We want to minimize the change in V(T) with respect to rates. To find that balance point, take the derivative of V(T) - Equation 2 - with respect to rates r and set it to 0.

$$dV(T) / dr = \text{sum}(i{=}1 \text{ to } N) \text{ of } \{ (T-i) * C(i) * (1+r)^{\wedge}(T-i-1) \} = 0$$
$$= \text{sum}(i{=}1 \text{ to } N) \text{ of } \{ C(i)* (1+r)^{\wedge}(-i) * (T-i) * (1+r)^{\wedge}(T-1) \} = 0$$
$$= \text{sum}(i{=}1 \text{ to } N) \text{ of } \{ PV(i)* [T * (1+r)^{\wedge}(T-1) - i * (1+r)^{\wedge}(T-1)] \} = 0$$

Setting one side equal to the other and dividing both by $(1+r)^{\wedge}(T-1)$
$$\text{sum}(i{=}1 \text{ to } N) \text{ of } \{ PV(i)* T \} = \text{sum}(i{=}1 \text{ to } N) \text{ of } \{ PV(i) * i \}$$

$$T = \text{sum}(i{=}1 \text{ to } N) \text{ of } \{ [PV(i) * i] \} / PV(0) \qquad \text{Equation 3}$$

That is, the time to hold the security to minimize the rate risk is T and is found by weighting present values by time.

Appendix to Chapter 9 - Sections A7a & A7b, Cont'd

In the 7 year bond example below, assume $(1+r)=$ 1.0101
Also assume an annual coupon of $5.750

i	C	PV (i)	From Equation 3 PV(i)*i / PV0	& Equation 2 C(i) * $(1+r)$ ^ (12-i)
1	$2.875	$2.846	0.023	$3.211
2	$2.875	$2.818	0.045	$3.179
3	$2.875	$2.790	0.067	$3.147
4	$2.875	$2.762	0.089	$3.116
5	$2.875	$2.734	0.110	$3.085
6	$2.875	$2.707	0.131	$3.054
7	$2.875	$2.680	0.151	$3.023
8	$2.875	$2.653	0.171	$2.993
9	$2.875	$2.626	0.190	$2.963
10	$2.875	$2.600	0.209	$2.933
11	$2.875	$2.574	0.228	$2.904
12	$2.875	$2.548	0.246	$2.875
13	$2.875	$2.523	0.264	$2.846
14	$102.875	$89.373	10.072	$100.828

Sum=PV(0)=   124.234

Sum=T=   11.996

V(T) = V(12) = $140.157

What would be our expected floor return if we held that time period? We want PV(0) and V(12). This is a 6 year period (12 semiannual).

$$PV(0)= \text{sum of the PV(i)'s} = \$124.234$$
$$\text{and } V(T)= \$140.157$$

The MINIMUM pre tax return we should get over the holding period is
$$[\ V(T) - PV(0)\ ]\ /\ PV(0) = \boxed{12.82\%}$$
This rate, expressed as an annual bey, compounded semi annually is $= 2.02\%$

Is it a minimum? Assume we hold for 12 periods and 1+r is actually different values. Below we see 1.01 is the floor.

(1+r)	V(T)
1.00	$140.25
1.01	$140.16
1.02	$140.26

What happens with multiple shifts, not just one?

There are two sectors, stocks and bonds
The fund is fully invested in the two asset classes.

Months	Fund Weight Stocks FW(1)	Fund Return Stocks FR(1)	Fund Weight Bonds FW(2)	Fund Return Bonds FR(2)	Index Weight Stocks IW(1)	Index Return Stocks IR(1)	Index Weight Bonds IW(2)	Index Return Bonds IR(2)
1	0.6	0.70%	0.4	0.50%	0.5	0.40%	0.5	0.20%
2	0.5	0.80%	0.5	0.60%	0.5	0.40%	0.5	0.20%
3	0.7	0.20%	0.3	1.20%	0.5	0.40%	0.5	0.20%
4	0.5	0.30%	0.5	0.60%	0.5	0.40%	0.5	0.20%
5	0.7	0.60%	0.3	-0.20%	0.55	0.40%	0.45	0.20%
6	0.1	0.40%	0.9	0.60%	0.55	0.40%	0.45	0.20%
7	0.3	0.50%	0.7	1.50%	0.55	0.40%	0.45	0.20%
8	0.4	0.80%	0.6	0.90%	0.55	0.40%	0.45	0.20%
9	0.9	0.50%	0.1	0.50%	0.55	0.40%	0.45	0.20%
10	0.3	0.20%	0.7	0.70%	0.6	0.40%	0.4	0.20%
11	0.2	0.90%	0.8	-0.60%	0.6	0.40%	0.4	0.20%
12	0.5	0.10%	0.5	0.40%	0.6	0.40%	0.4	0.20%

Fund Return FW(i)*FR(i) (A)	Fund Weights & Index Returns FW(i)*IR(i) (B)	Index Return IW(i)*IR(i) (C)	Bottom Up A-B	Top Down B-C	A-B + B-C = A-C
0.62%	0.32%	0.30%	0.30%	0.02%	0.32%
0.70%	0.30%	0.30%	0.40%	0.00%	0.40%
0.50%	0.34%	0.30%	0.16%	0.04%	0.20%
0.45%	0.30%	0.30%	0.15%	0.00%	0.15%
0.36%	0.34%	0.31%	0.02%	0.03%	0.05%
0.58%	0.22%	0.31%	0.36%	-0.09%	0.27%
1.20%	0.26%	0.31%	0.94%	-0.05%	0.89%
0.86%	0.28%	0.31%	0.58%	-0.03%	0.55%
0.50%	0.38%	0.31%	0.12%	0.07%	0.19%
0.55%	0.26%	0.32%	0.29%	-0.06%	0.23%
-0.30%	0.24%	0.32%	-0.54%	-0.08%	-0.62%
0.25%	0.30%	0.32%	-0.05%	-0.02%	-0.07%
6.27%		3.71%	2.73%	-0.17%	< Sums

Fund - Index Return =	**2.56%**	Sum (A-C) = Alpha	**2.56%**

Appendix to Chapter 9 - Section D1a

Open form option pricing -The hedging approach

Suppose one believed that assets could be two different levels in the future
(based on volatility and the forward). Could one hedge that with options?
If we sold calls, what is the hedge ratio so that you got the same ending
value in both cases? That would mean you were hedged.

Step 1 Set expiration ending values equal regardless of market movement

$h * P1 - MAX (P1 - K,0) = h * P2 - MAX(P2 - K,0)$
or $h = (MAX (P1 - K, 0) - MAX(P2 - K,0)) / (P1 - P2)$

h = hedge ratio (to solve for)
P1 = Asset Price in the future in state 1
K = Call strike price
P2 = Asset Price in the future in state 2

Step 2 Present value one ending value to get option price today

$(h*P1 - MAX (P1 - K,0)) / (1+r) = h*P0 - C0$

C0 = sold call premium (to solve for)
r = rate for assets that have no market risk in the future
P0 = Asset Price at time 0

Example

Step 1	Step 2
P1 = 101 K = 100 P2 = 99 P0 = 100	r = .002 = .2/100 = .2% P0 = 100
h = (1 - 0)/2 h = .5	C0 = 50 - ((50.5 - 1) / (1.002)) ; C0 = 0.5988

We have sold a 1 period option and to buy it back today would cost $0.5988

But are we hedged? Consider the end value defined in Step 2.
(h*P1 - MAX (P1 - K,0)) Below shows we have the same value with P1 and P2.

For P1, .5*101 - MAX (101 - 100, 0) = 49.5
For P2, .5*99 - MAX (99 - 100, 0) = 49.5

Appendix to Chapter 9 - Section D1b

Open form option pricing with continuous ending periods. Suppose:
1. You want to calculate the cost of a one year European call option on a 30 year bond.
2. The current price is $99.5 per $100 par. This is also the call "strike price".
3. The bond accrued is $.25 (we are just past a coupon date)
4. The coupon is 5% and the borrowing cost is 4%.
5. The day count convention for the bond coupon is 30/360 and the borrowing cost is actual/360.
6. The Discount Factor is from the borrowing cost pv*(1.04) = FV. Thus, DF = 1/1.04 = .9615
7. The standard deviation is 8%.

Step one. Calculate a forward price given we borrow $99.75 (Price + accrued) today.
1. Money to be earned from coupon = par * coupon rate * time (using day count convention)
   = $100 * .05 * 360 / 360 = $5.
2. Money to be paid to borrow money to buy the bond = (P+A) * borrowing rate * time
   = $99.75 * .04 * 365/360 = $4.0454
3. So, today we borrow $99.75. Over the term, we earn the coupon & pay the financing costs.
   Forward Price =$99.75 + $4.0454 - $5 = $98.7954 = Where we center the distribution.
4. Proof forward price is correct
   In one year, we deliver the bond and get $98.7954. We earn $5 on the coupon = $103.7954.
   We pay borrowing costs of $4.0454 and have $99.75 to pay back amount initially borrowed.
5. So, FP = Spot (P+A) + Borrowing Cost - Coupon earned.

Step two. Spread a distribution about the forward price.
1. Assume prices form a symmetric distribution (not a Black Scholes assumption but we will
   get there).
2. Assume the symmetric distribution is normal. This means approximately 66 2/3% of the
   scores will lie within one standard deviation of the mean.
3. Volatility is the standard deviation and is a percent of the forward price.

Step three. Define expiration payoffs and associated probability of the payoffs.

Step four. Present value probability weighted payoffs across forward prices and sum.
   The option premium is about $2.56 per $100 par paid today.

Y Axis

0.3989	X
0.242	X
Probability of X	
0.054	X
0.0044	X

X Axes	-3 Std Dev	-2 Std Dev	-1 Std Dev	The Fwd
Probability of X (Standard Normal Distribution)	0.0044	0.054	0.242	0.3989
Cumulative Probabilities of X	0.0044	0.0584	0.3004	0.6993
Forward Prices	75.0954	82.9954	90.8954	98.7954
Payoffs at Expiration (call struck at 99.5)	0.0000	0.0000	0.0000	0.0000
Probability * Option Payoffs	0.0000	0.0000	0.0000	0.0000
Present Value of Probability * Payoffs	0.0000	0.0000	0.0000	0.0000

Option Premium is the Sum = 2.5554

Y Axis

0.3989	
0.242	X
Probability of X	
0.054	X
0.0044	X

X Axes	1 Std Dev	2 Std Dev	3 Std Dev
Probability of X (Standard Normal Distribution)	0.242	0.054	0.0044
Cumulative Probabilities of X	0.9413	0.9953	0.9997
Forward Prices	106.6954	114.5954	122.4954
Payoffs at Expiration (call struck at 99.5)	7.1954	15.0954	22.9954
Probability * Option Payoffs	1.7413	0.8152	0.1012
Present Value of Probability * Payoffs	1.6743	0.7838	0.0973

Appendix to Chapter 9 - Section D1c

Open form option pricing - The Binomial Approach

1. Cox and Rubinstein (1985) presented the following analysis.

Assume we own a stock and bond portfolio. If we are all in stock, we replicate a deep in the money call.

If we are in bonds that earn a sure rate (riskless) rate over the period, we are indifferent to the market like an out of the money call.

So, we can replicate a call varying the amount of stocks and bonds.

Let:

[1] $h * (1+u) * S + B * (1+r) = Cu$
[2] $h * (1+d) * S + B * (1+r) = Cd$

h = the amount of stock held in the two states = the hedge ratio mentioned above.

u = stock upward movement. For example .01

d = stock downward movement. For example -.01

S = stock price before the movement

B = the amount held in bonds

r = the riskless interest rate over the time period the move takes place

Cu = worth of Call in up scenario

Cd = worth of call in down scenario

Since h is an unknown but the same value in both equations, we can subtract [1] - [2].

[3]   [1]-[2] = Cu-Cd = h*(1+u)*S - h*(1+d)*S ; h = (Cu - Cd) / (((1+u)-(1+d))*S

Or h=(Cu - Cd) / ((u-d) * S)

h = the change in the option price/the change in the stock price = the "delta".

We want to get an expression for B, the amount of cash we must hold. From [1] we have

[4]   h * (1+u) * S + B * (1+r) = Cu

Inserting h, ((Cu-Cd)/ ((u-d)*S)) * (1+u) * S + B * (1+r) = Cu

B*(1+r)= (Cu * (u-d)/(u-d)) - (Cu +u*Cu -Cd -u*Cd) / (u-d)

Or B = ((1+u)*Cd - (1+d)*Cu) /((u-d) * (1+r))

We now have expressions for h and B, the amount of stock and cash we need to replicate the call. We want C0 (the call worth "today"). At the prior node to the current up or down node, we have

[5]   C0 = S * h + B

C0 = (Cu-Cd)/(u-d) + ((1+u)*Cd - (1+d)*Cu) / ((u-d) *(1+r))

The numerator terms of the right side over a common denominator of (u-d)*(1+r) is:

(1+r)*Cu - (1+r)*Cd + (1+u)*Cd - (1+d)*Cu

Collecting terms

C0 = ((r-d)*Cu + (u-r)*Cd) / ((u-d) * (1+r))

[6]   C0 = [((r-d)/(u-d)) * Cu + ((u-r) / (u-d)) * Cd] / (1+r)

If we define the multiplier of Cu as P, the multiplier of Cd is 1-P since

P = (r-d)/(u-d) AND 1-P = (u-d) / (u-d) – (r-d) / (u-d) = (u-r)/(u-d)

We can write [6] as

[7]   C0 = (P * Cu + (1-P) * Cd) / (1+r)

2. For example

Stock Price	100.000000	
Call Strike	100.000000	
1+r	1.000027	(1+.01/365)
1+u	1.010000	
1+d	0.990000	
P	0.501370	
1-P	0.498630	

Steps
1. Calculate matrix of Stock Prices
2. Get ending call prices
3. Use above equation [7] for call prices
4. The matrix is continued on
   the next page

	0
Stock Price	100.00
C0 Price	**0.75**

	1(d)
Stock Price	99.00
Call Price	0.25

	2(dd)
Stock Price	98.01
Call Price	0.00

	2(du or ud)
Stock Price	99.99
Call Price	0.50

	3(ddd)
Stock Price	97.03
Call Price	0.00

	3(udd)
Stock Price	98.99
Call Price	0.00

3. Using the binomial probability distribution for short periods

# of Ups = U	N! / (N-U)! U!	P ^ U	(1-P)^(N-U)	Call Terminal Value =Max(S-K,0)	Probability times Terminal Value
	N=	3			
	(1+r) ^ 3 =	1.0001			
0	1	1.0000	0.1240	0.0000	0.0000
1	3	0.5014	0.2486	0.0000	0.0000
2	3	0.2514	0.4986	0.9899	0.7445
3	1	0.1260	1.0000	3.0301	1.1457
				C0 =	**1.8900**

1(u)	
Stock Price	101.00
Call Price	1.26

2(uu)	
Stock Price	102.01
Call Price	2.01

3(uud)	
Stock Price	100.99
Call Price	0.99

3(uuu)	
Stock Price	103.03
Call Price	3.03

4. Using it for longer periods - a thirty day option

	Stock Price	100.000	P	0.501
	Call Strike	100.000	1-P	0.499
	1+r	1.000	N	30.000
	1+u	1.010	(1+r) ^ N	1.001
	1+d	0.990		

				CO =	2.22

# of Ups = U	N! / (N-U)! U!	P ^ U	(1-P)^(N-U)	Call Terminal Value =Max(S-K,0)	Probability times Terminal Value
0	1	1.0000	0.0000	$0.00	$0.00
1	30	0.5014	0.0000	$0.00	$0.00
2	435	0.2514	0.0000	$0.00	$0.00
3	4,060	0.1260	0.0000	$0.00	$0.00
4	27,405	0.0632	0.0000	$0.00	$0.00
5	142,506	0.0317	0.0000	$0.00	$0.00
6	593,775	0.0159	0.0000	$0.00	$0.00
7	2,035,800	0.0080	0.0000	$0.00	$0.00
8	5,852,925	0.0040	0.0000	$0.00	$0.00
9	14,307,150	0.0020	0.0000	$0.00	$0.00
10	30,045,015	0.0010	0.0000	$0.00	$0.00
11	54,627,300	0.0005	0.0000	$0.00	$0.00
12	86,493,225	0.0003	0.0000	$0.00	$0.00
13	119,759,850	0.0001	0.0000	$0.00	$0.00
14	145,422,675	0.0001	0.0000	$0.00	$0.00
15	155,117,520	0.0000	0.0000	$0.00	$0.00

16	145,422,675	0.0000	0.0001	$1.87	$0.25
17	119,759,850	0.0000	0.0001	$3.93	$0.44
18	86,493,225	0.0000	0.0002	$6.02	$0.49
19	54,627,300	0.0000	0.0005	$8.17	$0.42
20	30,045,015	0.0000	0.0010	$10.35	$0.30
21	14,307,150	0.0000	0.0019	$12.58	$0.17
22	5,852,925	0.0000	0.0038	$14.86	$0.08
23	2,035,800	0.0000	0.0077	$17.18	$0.03
24	593,775	0.0000	0.0154	$19.54	$0.01
25	142,506	0.0000	0.0308	$21.96	$0.00
26	27,405	0.0000	0.0618	$24.42	$0.00
27	4,060	0.0000	0.1240	$26.94	$0.00
28	435	0.0000	0.2486	$29.50	$0.00
29	30	0.0000	0.4986	$32.12	$0.00
30	1	0.0000	1.0000	$34.78	$0.00

Appendix to Chapter 9 - Section D2

1. The Black-Scholes Equation for European calls on stocks with no dividends

	For example
S(t) = Stock price today	100.0000
T-t= time (in years) from today (t) to option expiration (T)	1.000000
r = the "riskless" interest rate (Libor) over period (T-t) Note: .01 = 1%	0.0100
K=Strike price	101.0000
vol=implied volatility	0.1900
d1 = (ln (S(t)/K) + (r + .5*vol^2) * (T-t))) / (vol * (T-t)^.5)	0.095261
N(d1) Note: N(d1) is the cumulative probability under the normal curve	0.537946
d2=d1 - vol * (T-t)^.5	-0.094739
N(d2)	0.462261

C(t) = S(t) * N(d1) - K * e^(-r*(T-t)) * N(d2)

$$\boxed{7.5708}$$

Noteworthy Excel Functions

N(d1) = .537946 = Normdist(d1,0,1,True)

N(d2) = .462261 = Normdist(d2,0,1,True)

1. The Black-Scholes Equation for European calls on stocks with no dividends

	For example
(from Chapter 9)	
S(t) = Stock price today	100.0000
T-t= time (in years) from today (t) to option expiration (T)	1.0000
r = the "riskless" interest rate (Libor) over period (T-t) Note: .01 = 1%	0.0100
K=Strike price	101.0000
vol=implied volatility	0.1900
d1 = (ln (S(t)/K) + (r + .5*vol^2) * (T-t))) / (vol * (T-t)^.5)	0.0953
N(d1) Note: N(d1) is the cumulative probability under the normal curve	0.5379
d2=d1 - vol * (T-t)^.5	-0.0947
N(d2)	0.4623
C(t) = S(t) * N(d1) - K * e^(-r*(T-t)) * N(d2)	7.5708

CP (Visual Basic) - See Appendix 10.C. =cp(0,100,101,.19,.01,1)	7.5708
PP (Put price - using the same parameters)	7.5658

Note that CP and PP are not exactly equal. Why are they even close?
What change in the above data would make CP and PP exactly equal?

Appendix to Chapter 10 - Sections A & B, Cont'd

2. Continuous dividends (at a dividend rate "cdr") creates two changes in Black-Scholes.

First, a "constant dividend a day" that is a percent of the base price is the same as compound interest, OR, $S(t) / e \wedge (cdr*(T-t)) = S(t)$ reduced by the dividends.

Second, d1 is effected. The "risk free rate" is reduced by the dividend rate.

Putting these together, we have

S(t) = Stock price today	100.0000
T-t= time (in years) from today (t) to option expiration (T)	1.0000
r = the "riskless" interest rate (Libor) over period (T-t) Note: .01 = 1%	0.0100
K=Strike price	101.0000
vol=implied volatility Note: .01 = 1%	0.1900
* **Dividend yield = cdr Note: .01 = 1%**	**0.0050**
* **d1 = (ln (S/K) + (r - cdr + .5*vol^2) * T)) / (vol * T^.5)**	**0.0689**
N(d1)	0.5275
d2=d1 - vol * T^.5	-0.1211
N(d2)	0.4518
* **C(t,cdr)=S(t) *e^(-cdr*(T-t)) * N(d1) - K * e^(-r*(T-t)) * N(d2)**	7.3051

Note   * means a change because of adding dividends

3. Early exercise of American Calls with dividends

Calls have time value. When you exercise, you lose time value.
Thus, if $S(t)-K >$ (Expected call premium), exercise early. OR

Early exercise can happen if FV of dividends > interest on strike. (See below).

Assume you buy the option at t. Time passes and you are at t'. The option expires at T.
Define r as the investment rate from t' to T.
Define D as the dividends, K as the strike and S as the security price.

	t	t'	T $S(T)<K$	T $S(T)=K$	T $S(T)>K$
Early exercise					
Pay strike		- K			
Get security			S(T)	S(T)	**S(T)**
Earn dividend			$D(T-t')*(1+r)$	$D(T-t')*(1+r)$	**$D(T-t')*(1+r)$**
Exercise **only at end**					
Call			0	0	**S(T) - K**
Invest the same at t'		- K	$K * (1 + r)$	$K * (1 + r)$	**$K * (1 + r)$**

Exercise early if Early > "only at end". The table shows that if the early exercise value
is greater than "only at end" when $S(T)>K$, it will be greater in the other states also.
This is because $S(T)-K$ is a positive number in that ending state. So, exercise early when

$$S(T) + D(T-t')*(1+r) > S(T) - K + K + K*r \text{ OR WHEN } D(T-t') > (K*r)/(1+r)$$

Early Exercise if D(T-t') * (1+r) > K * r OR D(T-t') > (K * r) / (1+r)

Matrix showing (K*r)/(1+r). D(T-t') must be greater for early exercise

	80	$0.00	$1.57	$3.08	$4.53
	60	$0.00	$1.18	$2.31	$3.40
K	40	$0.00	$0.79	$1.54	$2.27
	20	$0.00	$0.40	$0.77	$1.14
	0	$0.00	$0.00	$0.00	$0.00
		0.00%	2.00%	4.00%	6.00%
			r (T-t')		

If one knew when these minimum D's occurred, one could "PV" and get the approximate
minimum incremental premium for American call options since these cells show
the minimum total future value of the gain if one early exercises.

Appendix to Chapter 10 - Sections A & B, Cont'd

4. Put/Call parity on European Options with no dividend

Assume you buy a call and sell a put and lend the present value of the strike price.
Both put and call are at the same strike you lend.
What do you have at expiration?

A long call pays $\max(S(T) - K, 0)$
A sold put pays $- \max(K - S(T), 0)$
The lent strike gives you K.

	$S(T) > K$	$S(T) = K$	$S(T) < K$
Call	$S(T) - K$	0	0
Put	0	0	$- (K-S(T))$
Strike	K	K	K
Result	$S(T)$	$K = S(T)$	$S(T)$

You have the value of the stock at time T with the package.
To avoid arbitrage, that means the values at time t are equal.

Buy stock at time t = sell put and buy call and lend strike
$- S(t) = P(t) - C(t) - PV(K)$ or

$P(t) - C(t) = PV(K) - S(t)$	**PUT-CALL PARITY**

Appendix to Chapter 10 - Sections A & B, Cont'd

4. The Black-Scholes Equation for European puts on stocks with no dividends

$P(t) = PV(K) - S(t) + C(t)$

S(t) = Stock price today	100.0000
T-t = time (in years) from today (t) to option expiration (T)	1.0000
r = the "riskless" interest rate (Libor) over period (T-t) Note: .01 = 1%	0.0100
K = Strike price	101.0000
C(t) =	7.5708
P(t) =	7.5658

5. Continuous dividends creates the following changes for puts. From 4,

$P(t,cdr) = PV(K) - S(t)*e^{(-cdr*(T-t))} + C(t,cdr)$

S(t) = Stock price today	100.0000
T-t= time (in years) from today (t) to option expiration (T)	1.0000
r = the "riskless" interest rate (Libor) over period (T-t) Note: .01 = 1%	0.0100
K=Strike price	101.0000
Dividend yield = cdr	**0.0050**
C(t,cdr) =	**7.3051**

$P(t,cdr) = PV(K) - S(t)*e^{(-cdr*(T-t))} + C(t,cdr)$ 7.7989

```
Function CP(DY, S, K, VOL, R, T)
'
 CP = call price (USD per share)
 DY = dividend yield (.01 = 1%)
 S = today's stock price (100=$100 per share)
 K = strike of option (100 = $100 per share)
 VOL = Implied volatility (.19 = 19%)
 R = security financing rate from today to option expiration (.01=1%)
 T = time from today to option expiration in years ( .25 = three months)
'
If T = 0 Then
    CP = Application.Max(0, S - K)
    GoTo 100
End If
'
EXDY = 2.71828183 ^ (DY * T)
EXR = 2.71828183 ^ (R * T)
'
D1 = (Application.Ln(S / K) + (R - DY + ((VOL ^ 2) / 2)) * T) / (VOL * T ^ 0.5)
D2 = D1 - (VOL * (T ^ (0.5)))
ND1 = Application.NormDist(D1, 0, 1, True)
ND2 = Application.NormDist(D2, 0, 1, True)
'
CP = (S * ND1 / EXDY) - (K * ND2 / EXR)
100 End Function
```

```
Function PP(DY, S, K, VOL, R, T)
'
If T = 0 Then
   PP = Application.Max(0, K - S)
   GoTo 100
End If
'
EXDY = 2.71828183 ^ (DY * T)
EXR = 2.71828183 ^ (R * T)
'
D1 = (Application.Ln(S / K) + (R - DY + ((VOL ^ 2) / 2)) * T) / (VOL * T ^ 0.5)
D2 = D1 - (VOL * (T ^ (0.5)))
NMD1 = Application.NormDist(D1 * (-1), 0, 1, True)
NMD2 = Application.NormDist(D2 * (-1), 0, 1, True)
'
PP = (K * NMD2 / EXR) - (S * NMD1 / EXDY)
100 End Function
```

Appendix to Chapter 11

Assume the following data for the basket of deliverable notes for the 10 year note future

a. December 2013 note future quote of 125-28+   (125 + 28.5/32 per 100 par)
b. The first three Treasury Securities in the futures basket ordered by **highest IRP** first

	Units	Treasury Securities		
		1	2	3
Coupon	Annual Interest as % of par	2.625	2	3.625
Maturity	6.5-10 yrs	8/15/20	7/31/20	2/15/21
Price	32nds	104-14+	100-06 1/4	110-27+
Yield	bey	1.942	1.97	2.057
Factor		0.8205	0.7873	0.8659
Implied Repo rate	IRP in % or 1 = 1%	**-0.3705**	-0.8030	-1.0446
Gross Basis	32nds	37.1157	34.6120	59.2218
Net Basis	32nds	5.7054	10.8442	15.5945

Where

Coupon = the semi annual payment of interest
Maturity = years from settlement that par is paid to buyer
Price = the notes price on settlement
Yield = the notes bond equivalent yield for that price
Factor = the futures factor for each note
Implied Repo rate = the annualized AOY or money market rate earned if you bought
the note and shorted the future.

The IRP Formula is basically (ending\$ - beginning\$) / beginning\$. More formally,
IRP = { [(F*FQ - CP) + (A1 + ReinCoup - A0)] / [CP + A0] } * (360/(T-t))

Referring to the numbers below,
IRP = { [(#1*#2 - #3) + (#4 + #5 - #6)] / [#3 + #6] } * (360 / #7)

Let's get the actual numbers	Treasury Securities		
	1	2	3
(1) Factor (F)	0.8205	0.7873	0.8659
(2) Futures Quote (FQ)	125.890625	125.89063	125.890625
(3) Note OR Cash Price (CP)	104.453125	100.19531	110.859375
Settlement date (t)	8/12/2013	8/12/2013	8/12/2013
Coupon date prior to settlement date	2/15/2013	7/31/2013	2/15/2013
Next coupon date after settlement date	8/15/2013	1/31/2014	8/15/2013
Assumed Futures Delivery Date (T)	12/31/2013	12/31/2013	12/31/2013
Coupon date prior to delivery date	8/15/2013	7/31/2013	8/15/2013
Next coupon date after delivery date	2/15/2014	1/31/2014	2/15/2014
(4) Accrued at delivery (A1) =	0.9844	0.8315	1.3594
Are any coupons paid from 8/12/2013 to 12/31/2013?	Yes	No	Yes
(5) ReinCoup = Paid Coupons + reinvestment=	1.3128	0.0000	1.8129
Forward rates for coupon reinvestment =	0.0003	0.0003	0.0003
(6) Accrued Interest assumed at settlement (A0) =	1.2907	0.0652	1.7825
(7) Days between Settlement and Delivery (T-t) =	141	141	141

IRP = { | (#1*#2 - #3) + (#4 + #5 - #6) | / | #3 + #6 | } * (360 / #7)

	IRP=	-0.00370	-0.00803	-0.01045

On to Basis Calculations:

Gross Basis (in 32/nds) = (CP - F*FQ)*32 =	**37.11575**	**34.61195**	**59.22185**
Borrowing rate (Actual cost to borrow to buy note) =	**0.00060**	**0.00060**	**0.00060**
Coupon money earned = (A1 + ReinCoup -A0) =	**1.00642**	**0.76630**	**1.38982**
Borrowing paid = (CP+A0)*Borrowing Rate*Days/360 =	**0.02485**	**0.02356**	**0.02647**

Net Carry (in 32/nds)=
Coupon money earned - Borrowing paid =   **31.41039**   **23.76778**   **43.62731**

Does Net Carry explain futures price? Yes if Net Basis 0.
Net Basis (in 32nds) = Gross Basis - Net Carry =
   Net Basis = Value of delivery options? =   **5.70536**   **10.84417**   **15.59454**

Note: If Net Basis is positive, (Cash Price - F*FQ) - Net Carry > 0
   OR Cash Price - Net Carry > F*FQ.
   That is, the future is priced lower than the cheapest to deliver would suggest.
   That is usually assumed to be because of the "delivery options".

1. What could make the future price below the spot price and carry - the delivery options.

The short (the one who delivers the note to the long future position) has the following options if they go to delivery:

a. The cheapest to deliver (CTD) could switch - the quality option.

This option can be valued by moving the yield of the basket parallel up and down and calculating new IRP's. If a different CTD results, the futures price will be below the price associated with the original CTD. This loss, multiplied by the associated probability of the rate move, defines the future value of the cost. Summing across a distribution of rate moves and present valuing each product of loss times probability gives value.

b. One can deliver the security any time during the delivery month - one of the timing options

Assuming the IRP (return you earn) is greater than the financing cost, delivery is assumed end of month. If it is less, beginning of the month. In practice, end of month is assumed and this option has little value.

c. The so called "wildcard put option" - the second timing option.

Futures stop trading at 3PM NY time but notes stop trading 9PM NY time.

Thus, it would seem the short can wait to buy the note and if the market dips, buy the note and deliver into the higher "frozen" futures level and close out the future. That is, the futures quote is fixed and one gets factor times futures quote which is greater than the cash note price if the market dips. Note/bond delivery would close out the futures position and one would have bought low and sold high.

But wait. Wouldn't the short future position have to be "naked" from 3 - 9PM
so one can buy the note on a dip? If so, and the market went up in price,
you wouldn't buy the note and future would open next day at a higher level.
A loss would result on the futures position.

One has to be short and buy a call (or series of calls) to have a wildcard put. A short and a
purchased call at the forward price is a put also struck at the forward. This is put-call parity.
So the wildcard option is really the cost of the short and a series of calls that cover the
delivery month. The calls are daily good for 6 hours and are struck at the 3PM closing price.

**d. The third timing option - Futures stop trading eight days before the end of the
month, fixing their level. Cash still trades those eight days and thus that price
isn't fixed.**

Eight of the last set of the clique calls (as described above) have the same strike.

2. Estimating the hedge ratio.

Prior to the last day, there is a gross basis. Thus, we have CP - F * FQ = Gross basis
Consider an instantaneous move in yield in the cheapest to deliver (CP).
We have CP' - F * FQ' = Gross basis'

Since the move was instantaneous, assume the two gross basis' the same. Thus we have
CP - F * FQ = CP' - F * FQ'. **So FQ - FQ' = (CP - CP') / F.** This shows the instantaneous
change in the futures quote for a change in yield in the cash market equals the change
in the CTD cash price for that yield change divided by the factor (of the CTD).

In the general case, we don't own the CTD and want to hedge it with futures. Assume our
note changes $.03 in price per $100 par for a basis point change in yield. Using the Dec 2013
data, we have the CTD = 2.625 of 8/15/20. The CTD Factor is .8205. Assume the CTD
changes $ .02 per $100 par per basis point change in yield. We have
FQ-FQ' = .02 / .8205 = $.024375.

This means for every $1 par of our note, we need to short .03 / .024375 (or $1.23077) par
of futures to make the price change of the future equal that of our note. If we had 1.25
million par of our note, that would be about 15 contracts (1,250,000 * 1.23077 / 100,000).
We divide by 100,000 since that is the size of the futures contract.

3. Estimating the cost of hedging.

With no time remaining, futures and cash must converge. There is no carry and no delivery
options left. Thus, in the end, it is assumed Factor * Futures Quote = cash price.
The gross and net basis' are zero.

In the example above, the gross basis is $.011599 ((104.4531-.8205*125.8906)/100) per
$1 par of the CTD. Assume the CTD and our note move parallel in yield.
The cost is 1,250,000 * 1.23077 * $.011599 = $17,844.
We pay this because the future is below cash (converges upward) and we are short.

4. Eurodollar futures

A Eurodollar future is quoted 100-AOY yield. Thus a 97 quote is 3% forward yield.

Assume you own a floating rate note and want to "fix" the rate. You lose if rates go down.
You "go long" the Eurodollar future. If rates end at 2% and you went long one contract
at 3%, you make $2,500 = $1,000,000 * .01 * 3/12.

5. Swaps

A swap has two legs - a fixed rate leg and a floating leg. The fixed rate leg is typically due
every six months and the floating leg every three months. Sometimes they are both due every
three months and the payments are netted since one pays one and is paid the other.

For example, a 10 year swap might have a fixed leg at 3% and the three month libor rate
paid quarterly. Suppose you received the fixed leg and paid the floating leg, how do you know
you got a fair deal?

As always, you try to see if another market is cheaper to create the same thing. For example,
suppose you fixed the floating leg. You shorted a strip of eurodollar futures. What rate do
you get? The answer is the compounded Eurodollar future rates. There would be 40,
3 month Libor forward rates in 10 years and the fixed leg is semi annual. So,

$$(1+ER1) * (1+ER2) * \ldots * (1+ER40) = (1+.03/2) ^ 20$$

That is, the future value of the futures strip equals the future value of the fixed leg.

Appendix to Chapter 11 - Cont'd

Understanding the prior swap discussion involves 2 steps. First, the combination of swap
floating leg and short futures strip creates a fixed rate leg. That fixed leg rate should
equal the swaps fixed leg or arbitrage would result. Thus, the fixed rate on the swap
should equal the compounded futures strip rate.

6. Swaptions

Swaps behave like bonds that one has financed to buy. The fixed leg is like the bond's coupons.
The floating leg is the financing rate one pays to buy the bond (assuming rolling three month
borrowing). Thus, swaptions are priced like normal bond options. Also, see caps below.

7. Caps, Floors

Suppose you buy a 6 month floor (or call) struck at 5% on a four year rate (although more
normal is a three month rate). At the end of 6 months, four year rates are 1%. A cap takes
the arithmetic difference (4%) and assuming a notional of 100 your payout would be $4
per year for 4 years. You would get $16.

A "receiver" swaption would present value the swap defined by the strike since that would be
the swap fixed rate you could demand. That is equal to $5 per year for 4 years PV'ed at 1%
or $19.51.

A put swaption, is the counter of a cap. Both are puts but have the above differences.

8. Exotics - use Monte Carlo pricing - Chapter 15

As shown above, put options can pay differently even though they are puts. Clearly, their
worth differs also. Monte Carlo pricing is how "exotic" payment patterns are priced.

As the Monte Carlo Chapter shows, as long as the Monte Carlo scenarios are calibrated
to the capital markets, this technique will price any payment pattern. Calibration means:

1. The average of the (say) one year forward rates/prices scenarios equals the forwards
   in the market. That is, spot plus net carry holds.
2. The spread of the (say) one year scenarios is what is implied by the implied volatility
   in the market.
3. The distribution of scenarios is consistent with the assumed distribution of the asset

If these conditions hold, each scenario defines a payoff in the future and a probability.
Present valuing the probability times the payoff and summing across scenarios is the worth.

Appendix to Chapter 12

1. **We want to solve for probability of survival, given the premiums. Just like with rates, we "bootstrap". Let:**

   $P(0,n)$ = the premium for an n period credit derivative
   $DF(0,n)$ = the n period discount factor
   $PS(0,n)$ = the probability of surviving n periods
   R = recovery if default = 40

   Since the sellers expected gain equals the buyers and to default in the "nth" period means we survived n-1, we have:
   Seller's expected value = Buyer's expected value OR

   $P(0,n) * [DF(0,1)*PS(0,1) + DF(0,2)*PS(0,2) + ... + DF(0,n)*PS(0,n)] =$

   $-P(0,n) * [DF(0,1)*PS(0,1) + DF(0,2)*PS(0,2) + ... + DF(0,n-1)*PS(0,n-1)]$
   $+ (100-R)*DF(0,n)*(1-PS(0,n))$

   Collecting terms, Let

   $A = (100-R)*DF(0,n)$
   $B = 2*P(0,n)*[DF(0,1)*PS(0,1)+DF(0,2)*PS(0,2) +..+ DF(0,n-1)*PS(0,n-1)]$
   $C = P(0,n)*DF(0,n) + A$

   $PS(0,n) = (A - B) / C$ for n>0.

   Note -- If n=1, this simplifies to $PS(0,1) = (100-R) / [P(0,1) + (100-R)]$

   To see the n=1 case, consider to trade means both sides
   think the deal is fair OR $ if survive = $ if default OR
   $PS(0,1) * DF(0,1) * P(0,1) = (1-PS(0,1)) *DF(0,1) * (100-R)$

   This simplifies to $PS(0,n) = (A - B) / C$

To get PS(0,1), PS(0,2) … we have to apply the "bootstrapping" process.
It is assumed P(0,n) - the credit derivative premium - is known from the market.
The DF(0,n) are also assumed from the market but are tricky. They should be
from rates at a spread to par corporates (or Libor) to reflect risk.

Period 1

P(0,1)	1	Both known
DF(0,1)	0.99	From market
R =	40	Assumed
PS(0,1)=	0.98361	Calculated

Period 1 Check

From above, Seller = P(0,1) * DF(0,1) * PS(0,1) = .9738
Buyer= - Seller=(100-R)*DF(0,1)*(1-PS(0,1))= .9738

	Seller	Buyer
Period 1	0.9738	0.9738

Period 2

P(0,2)	1.25	Both known
DF(0,2)	0.985	From market
PS(0,2)	0.93924	Calculated

	Seller	Buyer
Period 1	1.2172	-1.2172
Period 2	1.1564	3.5909
Cumulative	2.3737	2.3737

Period 3

P(0,3)	1.5	Both known
DF(0,3)	0.97	From market
PS(0,3)	0.88011	Calculated

	Seller	Buyer
Period 1	1.4607	-1.4607
Period 2	1.3877	-1.3877
Period 3	1.2806	6.9773
Cumulative	4.1290	4.1290

The buyer and seller have equal expected values.

Suppose default happens in two periods but you did a 3 year trade

Results in Period 2 if a **3 year credit default swap** was transacted

Period 2

Seller = -(100-R) * DF(0,2) * (1-PS(0,2))

Buyer = (100-R) * DF(0,2) * (1-PS(0,2))

	Seller	Buyer
Period 1	1.4607	-1.4607
Period 2	-3.5909	3.5909
	-2.1302	**2.1302**

Results in Period 2 if a **2 year credit default swap** was transacted

Period 2

Seller = -(100-R) * DF(0,2) * (1-PS(0,2))

Buyer = (100-R) * DF(0,2) * (1-PS(0,2))

	Seller	Buyer
Period 1	1.2172	-1.2172
Period 2	-3.5909	3.5909
	-2.3737	**2.3737**

The buyer gains more (2.3737 > 2.1302) if the risk period = insured period.

2. Suppose you want premium (P), given probability of survival (PS).

Let A = (100-R)*DF(0,n)*(1-PS(0,n))

Let B = DF(0,1)*PS(0,1) + DF(0,2)*PS(0,2) + ... + DF(0,n-1)*PS(0,n-1)

Let C = DF(0,n)*PS(0,n)

Then P(0,n) = A / (2*B + C)

In the three period example on the prior page,

A= 6.9773

B= 1.8989

C= 0.8537

P(0,3)= 1.5000

The three year premium is $1.5 per year. See Period 3 on prior page.

Appendix to Chapter 13A

13A2a. Equity hedge ratios of two funded assets

**Only if Beta is measured using raw returns (R Beta)
does the widely used formula hold -**

HR1 = (MV2 / MV1) / **R Beta** (1 to 2)

The raw Beta (R Beta) is measured plotting pairs of typically monthly return points.
Asset 1 returns are on the Y axis and Asset 2 on the X axis. The slope of the
best fitting line gives you the change in return of Asset 1 to Asset 2.

Note that R Beta (1 to 2) is typically referred to as "Asset1 's Beta" only if Asset2
is the market. Here we use the term Beta slightly loosely to allow for generality.

Beta of Asset1 (relative to Asset2 or the market) in CAPM is
R1 = Risk Free Rate + **E Beta** (1 to 2) * (R2 - Risk Free Rate)
Where E Beta is Beta using excess returns or (R2 - Risk Free Rate)

For example,		Mean Return (over a period)	Risk Free Rate
Asset #	Value		
1	$1,000,000.00	5.00%	2.00%
2	$3,000,000.00	3.50%	2.00%

$$P1 = MV1*R1 = \quad \$50,000.00$$
$$P2 = MV2*R2 = \quad \$105,000.00$$

Hedge Ratio using raw Beta	
HR1 = P2 / P1	2.100
R Beta (1/2) estimated by 5% / 3.5%	1.429
HR1 = (MV2 / MV1) /R Beta(1/2)	**2.100**
Hedge Ratio using excess Beta	
E Beta (1/2) is estimated by 5% / (3.5%-2%)	3.333
HR1 = (MV2 / MV1) / E Beta(1/2)	0.900
Clearly, the hedge ratios are different	
Using the hedge ratio with raw beta, you need 2.1*1 M = 2.1 million of Asset1 to match the price change of Asset 2.	

Check
2.1 * 1 * 5%= 3 * 3.5% ;   0.105=0.105

Appendix to Chapter 13A, Cont'd

13A2b. Equity hedge ratios using futures

The most widely used future to hedge a portfolio is the S&P 500 future. One "regular" future changes $500 for one point move in the S&P 500 level (The E-mini future changes $250). Sticking with the regular (larger) future, one future is equivalent to having $800,000 in the market (1,600 * $500) with the S&P at 1,600.

To check that the price change of the future is equivalent to an $800,000 S&P portfolio of funded stocks, assume the $800,000 S&P portfolio moves 1% in return. That is $8,000. If the future at 1,600 index level moves 1%, that is 16 points. Since the futures payoff is $500 * point change, the future pays off $8,000.

The arithmetic in the prior section holds with futures.

For example, assume			Mean	Risk Free
Asset #	Value		Return	Rate
1	$2,300,000.00		2.00%	2.00%
2 (The future)	$800,000.00		1.00%	2.00%

R Beta(1/2) = 2%/1%=2,   So HR1 = (MV2 / MV1) /R Beta(1/2) = 0,174
Check >> .174 * $2,300,000 * .02 = $800,000 * .01

13A2c. Equity hedge ratios using options

When we use options to hedge, we must assume an investment horizon. If the horizon is very short, we must calculate the option change in value relative to the portfolio. This is called "delta hedging". One matches the deltas of the two assets (other Greeks also?)

If longer time horizons are chosen, the hedge ratio is as it is outlined above. That is, it is assumed you hold to option expiration and then the option is either In The Money or zero. If ITM, it acts like a security (the delta is 1). If out of the money, the hedge ratio is irrevalent - the option expired worthless and amount is irrevalent.

Appendix to Chapter 14 (1/4) - Sections A & B

					As of	1/31/2014
					Legal Final	1/31/2021
			Legal Final Remaining Term (Months)			84
				WAM (Months)		60
		Amortize to (1) Final Term or (2) Average				2
			Months used to Amortize Pool			**60**
			Initial Balance at as of date			$1,000,000.00
				Servicing per year		0.50000
			Prepayment (CPR) per year			5
				Assumed Recovery		40%
				WAL (Years)		**2.372**

1	2	3	4	5	6	7
	Collateral		Percent	Percent	Pool Balance at	Default occurs
Month	WAC	CPR	Deferred	Defaulted	End of Period	at beginning
0	(Annual)	(Annual)	per period	per period	**$1,000,000.00**	of the Period
1	4.000	5.0000	0	0	$980,715.83	$0.00
2	4.000	5.0000	0	0	$961,528.12	$0.00
3	4.000	5.0000	0	0	$942,436.45	$0.00
4	4.000	5.0000	0	0	$923,440.39	$0.00
5	4.000	5.0000	0	0	$904,539.54	$0.00
6	4.000	5.0000	0	0	$885,733.45	$0.00
7	4.000	5.0000	0	0	$867,021.73	$0.00
8	4.000	5.0000	0	0	$848,403.94	$0.00
9	4.000	5.0000	0	0	$829,879.69	$0.00
10	4.000	5.0000	0	0	$811,448.55	$0.00
11	4.000	5.0000	0	0	$793,110.11	$0.00
12	4.000	5.0000	0	0	$774,863.97	$0.00
13	3.750	5.0000	0	0	$756,635.16	$0.00
14	3.750	5.0000	0	0.1	$737,762.82	$756.64
15	3.750	5.0000	0	0.1	$719,021.82	$737.76
16	3.750	5.0000	0	0.1	$700,411.40	$719.02
17	3.750	4.7500	0	0.1	$682,080.18	$700.41
18	3.750	4.7500	0	0.1	$663,870.02	$682.08
19	3.750	4.7500	0	0.1	$645,780.27	$663.87
20	3.750	4.7500	3	0.1	$628,382.40	$645.78
21	3.750	4.7500	3	0.1	$611,083.37	$628.38
22	3.750	4.7500	3	0.2	$593,287.93	$1,222.17
23	3.750	4.7500	3	0.2	$575,624.59	$1,186.58
24	3.750	4.7500	3	0.2	$558,092.25	$1,151.25

POOL OF LOANS

8	9	10	11	12	13	14
Pool Balance After Default	Gross Interest Due After Default	Servicing Due After Default	Net Interest Due After Default	Net Interest After Default & Deferrment	Capitalized Interest After Default & Deferrment	Month
						0
$1,000,000.00	$3,333.33	$416.67	$2,916.67	$2,916.67	$0.00	1
$980,715.83	$3,269.05	$408.63	$2,860.42	$2,860.42	$0.00	2
$961,528.12	$3,205.09	$400.64	$2,804.46	$2,804.46	$0.00	3
$942,436.45	$3,141.45	$392.68	$2,748.77	$2,748.77	$0.00	4
$923,440.39	$3,078.13	$384.77	$2,693.37	$2,693.37	$0.00	5
$904,539.54	$3,015.13	$376.89	$2,638.24	$2,638.24	$0.00	6
$885,733.45	$2,952.44	$369.06	$2,583.39	$2,583.39	$0.00	7
$867,021.73	$2,890.07	$361.26	$2,528.81	$2,528.81	$0.00	8
$848,403.94	$2,828.01	$353.50	$2,474.51	$2,474.51	$0.00	9
$829,879.69	$2,766.27	$345.78	$2,420.48	$2,420.48	$0.00	10
$811,448.55	$2,704.83	$338.10	$2,366.72	$2,366.72	$0.00	11
$793,110.11	$2,643.70	$330.46	$2,313.24	$2,313.24	$0.00	12
$774,863.97	$2,421.45	$322.86	$2,098.59	$2,098.59	$0.00	13
$755,878.53	$2,362.12	$314.95	$2,047.17	$2,047.17	$0.00	14
$737,025.06	$2,303.20	$307.09	$1,996.11	$1,996.11	$0.00	15
$718,302.80	$2,244.70	$299.29	$1,945.40	$1,945.40	$0.00	16
$699,710.99	$2,186.60	$291.55	$1,895.05	$1,895.05	$0.00	17
$681,398.10	$2,129.37	$283.92	$1,845.45	$1,845.45	$0.00	18
$663,206.15	$2,072.52	$276.34	$1,796.18	$1,796.18	$0.00	19
$645,134.49	$2,016.05	$268.81	$1,747.24	$1,694.82	$52.42	20
$627,754.02	$1,961.73	$261.56	$1,700.17	$1,649.16	$51.01	21
$609,861.20	$1,905.82	$254.11	$1,651.71	$1,602.16	$49.55	22
$592,101.35	$1,850.32	$246.71	$1,603.61	$1,555.50	$48.11	23
$574,473.35	$1,795.23	$239.36	$1,555.87	$1,509.19	$46.68	24

POOL OF LOANS

15	16	17	18	19	20	21	22
Scheduled Principal Due After Default	Unscheduled Principal Due After Default	Deferred Principal After Default	Principal Recovered From Default	Total Principal After Default & Deferrment	Total Principal and Interest for Tranches	Principal Left At End of Period	Month
						$1,000,000.00	0
$15,083.19	$4,200.98	$0.00	$0.00	$19,284.17	$22,200.84	$980,715.83	1
$15,068.92	$4,118.79	$0.00	$0.00	$19,187.71	$22,048.13	$961,528.12	2
$15,054.66	$4,037.01	$0.00	$0.00	$19,091.67	$21,896.13	$942,436.45	3
$15,040.41	$3,955.64	$0.00	$0.00	$18,996.05	$21,744.83	$923,440.39	4
$15,026.18	$3,874.68	$0.00	$0.00	$18,900.86	$21,594.23	$904,539.54	5
$15,011.96	$3,794.12	$0.00	$0.00	$18,806.08	$21,444.32	$885,733.45	6
$14,997.76	$3,713.97	$0.00	$0.00	$18,711.73	$21,295.11	$867,021.73	7
$14,983.57	$3,634.21	$0.00	$0.00	$18,617.78	$21,146.60	$848,403.94	8
$14,969.39	$3,554.86	$0.00	$0.00	$18,524.26	$20,998.77	$829,879.69	9
$14,955.23	$3,475.91	$0.00	$0.00	$18,431.14	$20,851.62	$811,448.55	10
$14,941.08	$3,397.36	$0.00	$0.00	$18,338.44	$20,705.16	$793,110.11	11
$14,926.94	$3,319.20	$0.00	$0.00	$18,246.14	$20,559.38	$774,863.97	12
$14,987.69	$3,241.11	$0.00	$0.00	$18,228.81	$20,327.40	$756,635.16	13
$14,955.43	$3,160.27	$0.00	$302.65	$18,418.36	$20,465.53	$737,762.82	14
$14,923.24	$3,079.99	$0.00	$295.11	$18,298.34	$20,294.45	$719,021.82	15
$14,891.12	$3,000.28	$0.00	$287.61	$18,179.00	$20,124.41	$700,411.40	16
$14,859.07	$2,771.75	$0.00	$280.16	$17,910.98	$19,806.03	$682,080.18	17
$14,830.33	$2,697.75	$0.00	$272.83	$17,800.91	$19,646.36	$663,870.02	18
$14,801.65	$2,624.23	$0.00	$265.55	$17,691.43	$19,487.62	$645,780.27	19
$14,773.02	$2,551.21	($519.73)	$258.31	$17,062.82	$18,757.64	$628,382.40	20
$14,757.89	$2,480.93	($517.16)	$251.35	$16,973.01	$18,622.17	$611,083.37	21
$14,728.30	$2,408.63	($514.11)	$488.87	$17,111.69	$18,713.85	$593,287.93	22
$14,699.07	$2,336.87	($511.08)	$474.63	$16,999.49	$18,554.99	$575,624.59	23
$14,670.21	$2,265.65	($508.08)	$460.50	$16,888.28	$18,397.47	$558,092.25	24

TRANCHES

Cusip

Total Tranche A | | XXXXX

$800,000.00	Insertion		
$100,000.00	Width	Tranche WAL	1.152
$700,000.00	Exhaustion	Paid Prin Sum	$100,000.00

22	23	24	25	26	27	28	29
		Principal	Period	1 Month		Interest	
Month	CPR	Balance	Principal	Libor	Spread	Rate	$ Interest
0		**$100,000.00**	Paid			(Annual)	per period
1	5.00	$100,000.00	$0.00	0.22	1.00	1.22	$101.67
2	5.00	$100,000.00	$0.00	0.22	1.00	1.22	$101.67
3	5.00	$100,000.00	$0.00	0.22	1.00	1.22	$101.67
4	5.00	$100,000.00	$0.00	0.30	1.00	1.30	$108.33
5	5.00	$100,000.00	$0.00	0.30	1.00	1.30	$108.33
6	5.00	$100,000.00	$0.00	0.30	1.00	1.30	$108.33
7	5.00	$100,000.00	$0.00	0.30	1.00	1.30	$108.33
8	5.00	$100,000.00	$0.00	0.32	1.00	1.32	$110.00
9	5.00	$100,000.00	$0.00	0.32	1.00	1.32	$110.00
10	5.00	$100,000.00	$0.00	0.32	1.00	1.32	$110.00
11	5.00	$93,110.11	$6,889.89	0.35	1.00	1.35	$112.50
12	5.00	$74,863.97	$18,246.14	0.35	1.00	1.35	$104.75
13	5.00	$56,635.16	$18,228.81	0.35	1.00	1.35	$84.22
14	5.00	$37,762.82	$18,872.34	0.35	1.00	1.35	$63.71
15	5.00	$19,021.82	$18,741.00	0.35	1.00	1.35	$42.48
16	5.00	$411.40	$18,610.42	0.35	1.00	1.35	$21.40
17	4.75	$0.00	$411.40	0.38	1.00	1.38	$0.47
18	4.75	$0.00	$0.00	0.38	1.00	1.38	$0.00
19	4.75	$0.00	$0.00	0.38	1.00	1.38	$0.00
20	4.75	$0.00	$0.00	0.38	1.00	1.38	$0.00
21	4.75	$0.00	$0.00	0.41	1.00	1.41	$0.00
22	4.75	$0.00	$0.00	0.41	1.00	1.41	$0.00
23	4.75	$0.00	$0.00	0.41	1.00	1.41	$0.00
24	4.75	$0.00	$0.00	0.44	1.00	1.44	$0.00

1. Scheduled principal after default at end of month (i)

Scheduled principal (i) = Loan Balance(i) * Scheduled Monthly Mortality(i)

$$smm(i) = 1 - \{ [(1+c)^m - (1+c)^i] / [(1+c)^m - (1+c)^{(i-1)}] \}$$
(Proof is too detailed for the scope of this book but see Excel below)

Where
$c = WAC(i) / 1200$
m = months used to amortize pool
i = 1,2,3, ... m (the period)
See Appendix 14A&B.

Month (i)	c	m	smm (i)	Loan Balance (i)	Scheduled Principal(i) = smm(i) * Loan Bal (i)
1	**0.003333**	**60**	**0.015083189**	**$1,000,000.00**	**$15,083.19**
2	0.003333	60	0.015365223	$980,715.83	$15,068.92
3	0.003333	60	0.015657013	$961,528.12	$15,054.66
.....					
60	0.003125	60	1	$19,472.54	$19,472.54

If we used the PMT function in Excel, we need to subtract out interest since PMT is principal and interest. Note that PMT is expressed as a negative from Excel so make it positive to subtract out interest.

The Excel code for Scheduled Principal(i) - See Column 15 of Appendix 14 A&B

1	$15,083.19	= - PMT(4/1200, 60, 1000000)	- 1000000*(4/1200)
2	$15,068.92	= - PMT(4/1200, 59, 980715.83)	- 980715.83*(4/1200)

2. Going from CPR to smm to define unscheduled principal payment

You compound the loss in principal each month (due to prepayment) to get annual loss. Thus, with CPR expressed annually, let cpr = CPR/100 (Convert to %), smm' = unscheduled smm

$(1-smm')^{\wedge}12 = 1 - cpr$
$(1-smm') = (1-cpr)^{\wedge}(1/12)$
$smm' = 1-(1-cpr)^{\wedge}(1/12)$

For example,
$0.00427 = 1 - (1 -.05)^{\wedge}(1/12)$
Less than 1/2% (.43%) are lost monthly if 5% are lost each year.

3. Unscheduled principal after default at end of month (i)

Unscheduled principal (i) = Loan Balance after scheduled payment(i) * smm'(i)
Where Loan Balance(i) is after scheduled payment(i)
        and smm'(i) is defined by CPR(i)

Month (i)	CPR(i)	smm'(i) (see above)	Loan Balance after scheduled payment(i)	Unscheduled Principal(i)
1	**5.000000**	**0.004265319**	**$984,916.81**	**$4,200.98**
2	5.000000	0.004265319	$965,646.91	$4,118.79
3	5.000000	0.004265319	$946,473.46	$4,037.01
.....				
60	4.500000	0.003829643	$0.00	$0.00

4. Tranche Principal

As the pool shrinks, the tranche becomes "active" starting at "insertion". It shrinks along with the pool between insertion and exhaustion.

Month (i)	Pool Prin Left (i)	Tranche Exhaustion	Pool Balance above Exhaustion	Tranche Width	Tranche Par (i)
			= Max (a-b,0)		= Min (c,d)
	a	b	c	d	e
v	$800,000.00	$700,000.00	$100,000.00	$100,000.00	$100,000.00
.....					
w	$799,000.00	$700,000.00	$99,000.00	$100,000.00	$99,000.00
......					
x	$701,000.00	$700,000.00	$1,000.00	$100,000.00	$1,000.00
......					
y	$700,000.00	$700,000.00	$0.00	$100,000.00	$0.00

In Excel, Tranche Par(i) = MIN (MAX (a(i) - b(i) , 0) , d(i))

Another way to think about tranche par is as a put spread that gives you the width as premium.

| Put 1 = Sold a | $800,000 | strike put (K1) |
| Put 2 = Bought a | $700,000 | strike put (K2) |

At expiration, Put 1 payout = -MAX(K1 - Pool Prin Left (i) , 0)
At expiration, Put 2 payout = MAX(K2 - Pool Prin Left (i) , 0)

Month (i)	Pool Prin Left (i)	At Expiration Sold Put 1	At Expiration Bought Put 2	Initial Put 1 + Put 2 Premium	Tranche Par (i)
					= b + c + d
	a	b	c	d	e
v	$800,000.00	$0.00	$0.00	$100,000.00	$100,000.00
.....					
w	$799,000.00	($1,000.00)	$0.00	$100,000.00	$99,000.00
......					
x	$701,000.00	($99,000.00)	$0.00	$100,000.00	$1,000.00
......					
y	$700,000.00	($100,000.00)	$0.00	$100,000.00	$0.00

Suppose we have monthly returns of stocks and bonds. What is the aggregate risk ?

	Stocks (1) Monthly returns	Bonds (2) Monthly returns (1=1%)
Month 1	1.000	-1.000
Month 2	-0.500	0.500
Month 3	1.500	-1.500
Means	0.667	-0.667
Stdev	0.850	0.850
(using n not n-1)		

Suppose we equally weighted the Standard deviations? We get
$$.5 * .85 + .5 * .85 = .85$$

That is not the risk of a 50/50 investment. For that we have

Month 1	.5 * (1) + .5 * (-1) =	0
Month 2	.5 * (-.5) + .5 * (.5) =	0
Month 3	.5 * (1.5) + .5 * (-1.5) =	0

The actual risk is 0, not .85

What measure takes into account the fact that the real risk is 0?
Var = weighted sum of the covariances. For two variables, we have
Var = w1*w1*Cov(1,1) + w1*w2*Cov(1,2) + w2*w1*Cov(2,1) + w2*w2*Cov(2,2)

	Cov (1,1) (x-mean x)*(x-mean x)	Cov(1,2) (x-mean x)*(y-mean y)	Cov(2,1) (y-mean y)*(x-mean x)	Cov(2,2) (y-mean y)*(y-mean y)
Month 1	0.1111	-0.1111	-0.1111	0.1111
Month 2	1.3611	-1.3611	-1.3611	1.3611
Month 3	0.6944	-0.6944	-0.6944	0.6944
Covariances =	0.7222	-0.7222	-0.7222	0.7222
(Average)				

Thus, Var =	0.5*0.5*(.722)+0.5*0.5*(-.722)+0.5*0.5*(-.722)+0.5*0.5*(.722)
	Std=SQRT(Var)= 0.00000

Now assume our mix is 1.0 Stocks and 0.0 Bonds. We have

Thus, Var =   1.0*1.0*(.722)+1.0*0.0*(-.722)+0.0*1.0*(-.722)+0*0*(.722)

        Std =   0.850

Note this standard deviation is and should be the answer for the 100% stock case (see above)

We thus have two points on our "efficient frontier" plot.		
	Point 1	Point 2
Weights >>	(.5, .5)	(1, 0)
Return	0	0.667
Risk (Std Dev)	0	0.850
An efficient frontier would use Excel Solver to maximize the return		
fixing the risk by narrowly constraining the weighted std dev.		

Appendix to Chapter 15 - Section B

A Monte Carlo Cookbook

A. The basic concepts

The basic matrix has assets as columns and 1+ period returns in the rows
    Each period return has a mean drift (due to time passage) and a variability.
    To be calibrated to the capital markets, the mean drift is net carry.
    The variability of a period return is the standard deviation times a random number.
    Random numbers are adjusted across assets (Cholesky decomposition) to reflect correlation
    between assets.

To create a scenario for one asset, select the appropriate number of rows to make up the time
required for the investment horizon. Starting with current levels, multiply each 1+period return
the prior number to create a series of levels over time for that asset and scenario.

As always in finance, the devil is in the details.

B. The devilish details

1. Define the set of assets of interest and their weights.
2. Define the time period that will be the smallest "step" in your scenarios (perhaps one month?).
3. Define the total period of interest (perhaps one year).
4. Define (in this case) the current yield and financing rates - assume a constant net carry.
5. Define the volatility using current implied volatility.
6. Draw random numbers that have mean 0, std 1.
7. If you believe the assets are correlated, adjust the random numbers (Cholsky decomposition).
8. Define the period returns (total or price only) using the Random Numbers from #7.
9. Apply the returns to the assets to get asset values over time.
10. Aggregate the scenario results and interpret them.

Appendix to Chapter 15 - Section B, Cont'd

C. An example:

1. **Assume 60% stocks, 30% bonds and 10% cash.**
2. **Choose monthly returns.**
3. **Total projection for one year.**
4. **Define (in this case) the current yield and financing rates - assume a constant net carry.**

Since (1+monthly return) ^12 = 1+annual return
monthly return=((1+annual)^(1/12)-1)

	Annual Financing	Annual Dividend	Mean drift = Monthly (Financing - Dividend)
Stocks (assume S&P 500)	3%	2%	0.0815%
Bonds	3%	4%	-0.0807%
Cash	3%	3%	0.0000%

5. **Define the volatility using current implied volatility.**

An implied price return volatility of 19% means that in one year, todays index should be + or - 19% from it's one year forward 66% of the time. That is, the distribution is assumed normal and + or - one standard deviation includes 66% of a normal curve.

Assuming the months are independent (see Section 9D2), we have:
Monthly price volatility = Annual price volatility/Sqrt(12)

	Annual Volatility	Monthly Volatility
Stocks (assume S&P 500)	19%	5.48%
Bonds	6%	1.73%
Cash	0.35%	0.10%

6. Draw random numbers that have mean 0, std 1.

Assuming you are using Excel, type in a cell =NORMINV(Rand(),0,1). Create 3 columns (stocks, bonds, cash). These numbers are from a population with Mean 0, Standard Deviation 1. The standard deviation uses n as the divisor (STDEVPA). For simplicity, we will use only six rows - two scenarios with three months each. **These are the Raw Random numbers.**

Scenario	Month	Stocks	Bonds	Cash
1	1	1.510751	1.014741	-1.053446
1	2	-2.039267	0.555708	0.121848
1	3	-0.321131	-0.468422	1.203123
2	1	-0.728251	0.910130	0.680526
2	2	-1.659875	0.555556	-0.475842
2	3	-0.215370	1.324391	1.285305

7. If the assets are correlated, adjust the random numbers (Cholsky decomposition).

Suppose you thought stocks and bonds returns were negatively correlated. The correlation was -1. To accomplish this in a Monte Carlo, you could multiply the random numbers of stocks by -1 and use those random numbers for the bonds. This is the idea behind a Cholsky decomposition.

Step 7.1. Define a target **correlation** matrix of the returns (usually using historical data). (If historical, use Excel Correl function. Otherwise, perhaps using expectations?)

Target Correlation Matrix			j = 1	2	3
			Stocks	Bonds	Cash
	1	Stocks			
i =	2	Bonds	-0.2		
	3	Cash	0.05	0.1	

Step 7.2. Calculate the Cholesky weight matrix

Where   a. First column

$C(1,1) = 1$

$C(2,1) = CORREL(2,1)$ (Bond monthly returns to stocks using Excel)

$C(3,1) = CORREL(3,1)$ ...

b. Cells on the diagonal (beyond first cell of diagonal)

For i=j;   **$C(i,j) = SQRT\{ 1 - SUM(k=1 \text{ to } i-1), [C(i,k)^2] \}$**

c. Interior

For i>j and C(j,j) > 0; $C(i,j) = (1/C(j,j)) *$
         $\{ CORREL(i,j) - SUM (k=1 \text{ to } j-1), [C(j,k)*C(i,k)] \}$

For i>j and C(j,j)<=0; $C(i,j) = 0$

Cholesky Weight Matrix			j = 1	2	3
(using the target correlation matrix)			Stocks	Bonds	Cash
	1	Stocks	1.000000		
i =	2	Bonds	-0.200000	**0.979796**	
	3	Cash	0.050000	0.112268	**1.00503939**

Note: With four variables, we have an expanded correlation matrix. The Cholesky is:

	Stocks	Bonds	Cash	Alternatives
Stocks	C(1,1)			
Bonds	C(2,1)	**C(2,2)**		
Cash	C(3,1)	C(3,2)	**C(3,3)**	
Alternatives	C(4,1)	C(4,2)	C(4,3)	**C(4,4)**

Step 7.3 Define the Non Adjusted (NA) random numbers - Combine the raw
random numbers with the Cholesky coefficients

$$NA(i,j) = \text{sum}(k=1 \text{ to } n) \text{ of } [\ RR(i,k)*C(j,k)\ ] \quad \text{where } n = \# \text{ of assets (here } n=3)$$

Scenario	Month	Stocks	Bonds	Cash
1	1	1.51075	0.69209	-0.86929
1	2	-2.03927	0.95233	0.08289
1	3	-0.32113	-0.39473	1.14054
2	1	-0.72825	1.03739	0.74972
2	2	-1.65987	0.87631	-0.49886
2	3	-0.21537	1.34071	1.42970

Step 7.4 Adjust the correlated numbers to mean = 0, stdev = 1.

First, divide each cell in a column by the standard deviation of that column. Each
columns standard deviation will now be 1.
Second, find the mean of each adjusted column.
Third, subtract the mean of each column from the numbers in the column.
The mean of the column will now be 0.
The result is a matrix of **Processed Random Numbers**. The columns are **Assets** and
the rows are **Scenarios** (at least 1,000 scenarios).

Scenario	Month	Stocks	Bonds	Cash
1	1	1.35004	0.70049	-0.82645
1	2	-1.82233	0.96389	0.07880
1	3	-0.28697	-0.39952	1.08432
2	1	-0.65078	1.04999	0.71277
2	2	-1.48330	0.88695	-0.47427
2	3	-0.19246	1.35698	1.35923

8. Define the period returns (total or price only) using the "Processed Random Numbers" from #7.

1 + Monthly Price Return =
    1 + (Monthly Net Carry + Monthly Std Dev of Price Returns * Processed Random Number)

1+ Monthly Total Return = 1 + (Monthly Net Carry +
    Monthly Dividend Yield + Monthly Std Dev of Total Returns* Processed Random Number)

Assume you choose to Monte Carlo total returns. The first 24 rows of 1 + returns might look like:

Scenario	Months	Stocks	Bonds	Cash	Scenario	Months	Stocks	Bonds	Cash
1	1	1.0760	1.0229	1.0078	2	1	0.9663	1.0289	1.0093
1	2	0.9020	1.0274	1.0087	2	2	0.9206	1.0261	1.0081
1	3	0.9862	1.0038	1.0097	2	3	0.9914	1.0343	1.0100
1	4	1.0682	1.0135	1.0089	2	4	1.0280	0.9850	1.0084
1	5	1.0423	1.0192	1.0098	2	5	0.9865	1.0261	1.0080
1	6	1.0044	1.0333	1.0084	2	6	0.9778	1.0141	1.0087
1	7	0.9685	0.9741	1.0069	2	7	1.0063	0.9939	1.0069
1	8	0.9367	1.0060	1.0085	2	8	0.9659	1.0212	1.0104
1	9	1.0501	0.9882	1.0076	2	9	1.0064	1.0156	1.0077
1	10	1.0315	1.0190	1.0103	2	10	1.0430	1.0257	1.0078
1	11	0.9452	0.9980	1.0096	2	11	1.0494	0.9587	1.0106
1	12	0.9542	1.0066	1.0070	2	12	1.0555	1.0257	1.0090

9. Apply the total returns to the assets to get asset values over time.
   (See Section C1 for starting values).

Scenario	Months	Stocks	Bonds	Cash	Sum
1	0	$60.00	$30.00	$10.00	$100.00
1	**1**	**$64.56**	**$30.69**	**$10.08**	**$105.33**
1	2	$58.23	$31.53	$10.17	$99.93
1	3	$57.43	$31.65	$10.26	$99.35
1	4	$61.35	$32.08	$10.36	$103.78
1	5	$63.94	$32.69	$10.46	$107.09
1	6	$64.22	$33.78	$10.54	$108.55
1	7	$62.20	$32.91	$10.62	$105.72
1	8	$58.26	$33.10	$10.71	$102.07
1	9	$61.18	$32.71	$10.79	$104.68
1	10	$63.11	$33.33	$10.90	$107.34
1	11	$59.65	$33.27	$11.01	$103.92
1	12	$56.92	$33.49	$11.08	$101.49
2	**1**	**$57.98**	**$30.87**	**$10.09**	**$98.94**
2	2	$53.37	$31.67	$10.18	$95.22
2	3	$52.92	$32.76	$10.28	$95.95
2	4	$54.40	$32.27	$10.36	$97.03
2	5	$53.66	$33.11	$10.45	$97.22
2	6	$52.47	$33.58	$10.54	$96.59
2	7	$52.80	$33.37	$10.61	$96.79
2	8	$51.00	$34.08	$10.72	$95.80
2	9	$51.33	$34.61	$10.80	$96.74
2	10	$53.53	$35.50	$10.89	$99.92
2	11	$56.18	$34.04	$11.00	$101.22
2	12	$59.30	$34.91	$11.10	$105.31

10. Aggregate the scenario results and interpret them.

10.1 Aggregate data from Monte Carlo

Months	0	1	2	3	4	5	6
Scenario							
1	100.00	$105.33	$99.93	$99.35	$103.78	$107.09	$108.55
2	100.00	$98.94	$95.22	$95.95	$97.03	$97.22	$96.59
Average value		$102.13	$97.58	$97.65	$100.40	$102.16	$102.57
Std dev		$3.19	$2.35	$1.70	$3.38	$4.93	$5.98

Months	7	8	9	10	11	12
Scenario						
1	$105.72	$102.07	$104.68	$107.34	$103.92	$101.49
2	$96.79	$95.80	$96.74	$99.92	$101.22	$105.31
Average value	$101.26	$98.94	$100.71	$103.63	$102.57	**$103.40**
Std dev	$4.47	$3.14	$3.97	$3.71	$1.35	**$1.91**

10.2 Interpretation

Assume an efficient frontier suggested the 60, 30, 10 weights over a period. If these Monte Carlo results were the results of 1000 + scenarios, the result would be you would make on average 3.4% + 1.91% or 3.4% - 1.91%.

EXERCISES

Exercises for Chapter 1

1 If you were an issuer, what questions would you ask before you raised money for a new project? Project questions and traditional market questions.

2 As an issuer, what aspects of the projects would make you choose (say) stocks instead of bonds?

3 If you were an issuer, what is the effect on your financials of raising money using traditional assets?

4 If you are an individual investor, would you buy traditional assets and put them in your broker account or would you buy mutual funds?

5 If you are a corporation, how would you invest differently in your different divisions - holding company, operating company, etc.?

6 Choose low, medium and high risk
   a. What are the different categories of risk you can think of (interest rate,?)
   b. How would you pool those categories to get one measure of risk?
   c. What traditional asset mix would you choose in the different risk levels to maximize return?

Exercises for Chapter 2

1 Assume the following data - do interest rate differentials explain the currency quote?

FX forwards are quoted in points. These are to be added or subtracted to
Spot to determine levels. When would points be added? When subtracted?
Hint: The rates need "help" from the currency levels.

	Points bid	Points offer	
1M	1.160	1.560	
2M	2.710	2.830	
3M	4.200	4.800	

	Levels bid	Levels offer	
Spot	1.3260	1.3260	USD/EUR
1M	1.3261	1.3262	USD/EUR
2M	1.3263	1.3263	USD/EUR
3M	1.3264	1.3265	USD/EUR

The Euro Investment. Do all "today"
1. Again start with $100 USD.
2. Spot convert to EURO
3. Invest in Euribor
4. Forward sell the Euro back to USD

1M	0.190%	0.200%	USD Libor
2M	0.230%	0.240%	USD Libor
3M	0.270%	0.270%	USD Libor

1M	0.131%	0.131%	Euribor Rate
2M	0.182%	0.182%	Euribor Rate
3M	0.228%	0.228%	Euribor Rate

For example, the one month future value is
100 USD / 1.3260 USD/EUR *
(1+.131%) * 1.3261 USD/EUR

US Dollar investments

1M	100.1900	USD Future Value	
2M	100.2300	USD Future Value	
3M	100.2700	USD Future Value	

The Euro results:

100.1398 USD Future Value	1M
100.2025 USD Future Value	2M
100.2597 USD Future Value	3M

The USD and Euro results are close for the same maturity.

2 Consider the Following Commodity Data for Dec 2013 Corn

Exch	Contract Size	Quote (Points)	$ per Point	Contract Value	per bushel
CBOT	5000 bushels	478	$50	$23,900	$4.78

a. How is contract value calculated?

b. A farmer wants protection for corn prices falling.
   He estimates he will grow 75,000 bushels and sell in Dec 13.
   Should he go long or short the future and how many?

c. After he trades, the futures go up to 480. How much has the trade made or lost him?

3 What would you look for in an ideal LBO candidate?

4 As a venture capitalist, what is your business plan to develop the following idea?

a. A new computer application that is like angry birds but involves frisby's.

b. A new type of steel.

5 What hedge fund would you run. Develop market material for your investor.

6 What are the risks in Mezzanine funds vs senior bond funds?

7 Create a structured note from a pool of

a. an "unfunded" security like a derivative

b. a "funded" security like a mortgage

c. What are the challenges/differences in the two different structured notes?

Exercises for Chapter 3

1 What is the difference between going long vs going short a forward?

2 Explain the difference between selling a call and buying a put
   option on the same stock.

3 Make a gain/loss graph at expiration of a sold call struck at 67.5.
   Graph from 60-70 on the X axis. Assume the call is bid 1.13
   and offered at 1.14.
   Assume current market for the underlying stock is 66.37.

4 Make a gain/loss graph at expiration of a long put struck at 67.5
   Assume the put is on the same stock as above. Graph from 60-70 on the
   X axis. Assume the put is bid 2.25 and offered at 2.27.
   Assume current market for the underlying stock is 66.37.

5 What is the intrinsic and time value of the above two positions?

6 What is the difference between American and European options?

7 What tests would you perform to see if the following futures are mis-priced?

   a. S&P 500 stock future
   b. Corn future
   c. Gold
   d. EuroDollar Future

Exercises for Chapter 3, Cont,d

8 Assume the following data

Bond maturity 2 years
Bond coupon 2%
Bond price $90
Bond accrued $2
Bond Par $100

Three month T-bill rate 1%
Three month Libor rate 1.5%
Your companies three month financing rate 1.75%
Two year Libor rates 1.9%

a. What is the probable fair market forward price?

Thus, Spot + financing - coupon = $89.845

Check - buy bond and sell forward
       -$92.000 Paid to buy bond
        -$0.345 Paid to finance bond ($92 * .015/4)
        $89.845 Price bond sold through forward sale
        $2.500 Accrued interest earned at sale
        $0.000 Sum

b. Should you enter into a forward or finance yourself?

Assume self financing doesn't significantly affect balance sheet.

Buy bond by self financing and sell forward in the market

-$92.000 Paid to buy bond

-$0.403 Paid to finance bond

$89.845 Price bond sold through forward sale

$2.500 Accrued interest earned at sale

-$0.058 Sum

Note - loss due to higher financing rate

$0.345 Market assumed cost

-$0.403 Company cost

-$0.058 Sum

9 **If the company is bullish on the bond, what should they do?**

10 **What should be the difference in a three month put and call premium struck at the forward price? What is equivalent to that position?**

11 **What are some other ways to generate the same payoff patterns at expiry?**

a. Long a forward and long a put struck at the forward.

b. Long a forward and sell a call at the forward.

c. Long a put and sell a call, both struck at the forward.

d. Long a forward, sell a put and buy a call both at the forward.

e. Long a call and sell a put, both 10 points OTM from spot

Exercises for Chapter 4

1. Describe the basic steps in Exchange execution.

2. Describe the credit risk exchange members take when they trade on behalf of their clients. How do exchange members mitigate that credit risk?

3. What are the pro's and con's of exchanges going to electronic execution?

4. What are the pro's and con's of exchange execution and the current "bi-lateral" OTC model?

5. Google Dodd-Frank. Is it creating an OTC market that has dealers "too big to fail? Do you think it is solving the 2008 issues?

6. Build your own execution system that is fair, transparent and economical.

7. What is the difference between hedging, speculation and arbitrage?

8. Compare OTC forwards and exchange traded futures contracts and list at least four differences.

9. In the Chicago Board of trade's corn futures contract, the following delivery months are available; March, May, July, September and December.

   State the contract that should be used for hedging when the expiration of the hedge (or target date) is a) April, b) July, c) January.

10. Does a perfect hedge lock in spot price or forward price or neither?

Exercises for Chapter 5

1. What futures position is similar to the following trades?
   a. Repo
   b. Reverse
   c. Lend

2. Suppose you were a corporate treasurer. You issue fixed rate debt.
   What trade would you do to protect yourself against rates rising
   and your debt costs increasing because you must pay a higher coupon
   for the same amount of proceeds coming from the issuance?

3. Suppose you are buying another company. What are your risks?
   How would you hedge those risks?

4. What are the risks associated with securities lending?
   Design a lending program to protect yourself against
   those risks.

5. What does the existance of swaps suggest about Libor?
   Is there only 3 month Libor or does it have varying maturities?
   If Libor has varying maturities, how are they linked to 3 month Libor?

6. Each of the following pays you if rates go down.
   What are the unique risks to each?
   a. Repo
   b. Long a future
   c. Receive fixed spot start
   d. Receive fixed forward starting
   e. Lend a security and invest in another security of longer maturity than the
      cash received from the lend.

7. Cash plus a future is a bond. Why? What is the maturity of the cash investment to make that true?

8. If cash plus a future is a bond, how does that relate to a Repo?

Exercises for Chapter 6

1. **Under what conditions would you want to buy credit default protection?**
   Under what conditions would you sell protection?
   Instead of buying protection, when would you just sell the security?

2. **In what ways is selling protection like securities lending?**

3. **In what ways is selling protection on a corporate bond and buying a treasury similar to buying a corporate bond? How are they different?**

4. **Assume the buyers (of protection) think the possibility of default is further away in time than the sellers. Assuming equilibrium pricing, in what ways does that affect the single period pricing equation?**

5. **You can buy protection "forward". That is, the period starts in the future and ends further in the future.**
   Assume four year premiums are $3 per $100. If one year premiums are $1, what is the fair on year forward for three years neglecting present values?

6. **When might you buy an option on buying or selling protection?**

Exercises for Chapter 7

1. List some factors why equity futures only go on in time for a short period.

2. Why do equity forwards/futures increase in price as time increases?

3. Name some factors why most academic pricing literature is stock related when corporations mainly buy bonds.

4. What is different about commodity forward pricing?

Exercises for Chapter 8

1. Structured paper requires a team to issue it. What do you think are the roles of the following players assuming the issuer is bringing a CMO deal to the market?

      a. Mortgage originator
      b. Broker / Dealer
      c. Rating Agency
      d. Trustee
      e. Securities Lawyer
      f. Investor

2. The normal yield curve is upward sloping - yields go up as maturities increase. How does that help explain how tranched structured paper is economical to produce?

3. Compare and contrast investing in mutual funds and investing in structured paper.

4. How is risk reduced in structured paper?

5. What are the advantages and disadvantages of pro-rata vs waterfall?

6. If you were the rating agency, what would cause you to rate a tranche highly?

7. As an investor buying tranched paper, what would you look for?

Exercises for Chapter 9

1. Why are future cash flows worth less today than the amount of the cash flow itself? Under what conditions would they be worth more?

2. Suppose you believe rates are going down tomorrow and stay down. Should you present value using today's rate or the lower rate of tomorrow?

3. Why don't equities have term structure?

4. What is the relationship between discount factors and forward rates? Prove it.

5. Describe the two basic properties of Macaulay duration. What are the limitations of using these concepts in the "real world".

6. Why is duration not used as a measure of risk with equities?

7. What is the difference between standard deviation and beta as risk measures?

8. Could bonds have betas?

9. Define a security and calculate all the return measures.

10. Define "top-down" and "bottom-up" measures of performance. How are the two measures calculated?

Exercises for Chapter 9, cont'd

11. What is the essence of the arbitrage argument in option pricing?

12. What are the six fundamental variables in option pricing?
    a. Which four essentially define the forward price?
    b. Which two are unique to option pricing?

13. Define the basic steps in the binomial approach to option pricing.

14. What must the means of the prices be at any point in time across scenarios to avoid arbitrage when using the binomial approach?

15. What are the factors of a bond that would reduce convexity?

16. An investor has $100,000 to invest.
    What will this grow to in one year at 10% using:

        a) annual compounding
        b) monthly compounding
        c) semi-annual compounding
        d) quarterly compounding
        e) continuous compounding

17. Why are the answers different in the above question?

Exercises for Chapter 10

1. The definition of expected value is to multiply a value times it's probability.
   Where is that concept used in Black-Scholes?

2. Why do European options present value the strike price K?

3. What is the most N(d1) can be? How about N(d2)?

4. Assuming continuous dividends is clearly not "the real world".
   How might that distort pricing?

5. Suppose the options are on a future. What should long call, short put both
   struck at the future price behave like? Is there a name for this?

6. What is the complication American calls introduce?

7. Why is it tough to estimate the incremental value of American calls?

8. The Chapter says you early exercise calls if D > (K * r) / (1+r) .
   Over what time period is D and r?

9. Under what conditions would the put and call be exactly the same price
   in Appendix 10 A&B?
   What change would you have to make to the example to make that so?

Exercises for Chapter 11

1. Why does one get factor times futures quote (plus accrued) when one delivers a note into the futures contract?
   What were the contract designers trying to do?

2. Why does the gross basis exist? Can it ever be negative?

3. What causes the difference between the Gross and Net Basis ?

4. What causes the Net Basis to be greater than zero?

5. In your words, define the IRP. How does it relate to the financing rate of the note?

6. What is the point of buying clique calls to value the wildcard delivery option?

7. Why is the change in the futures value approximated by the change in the CTD divided by the factor?

8. If you were a hedger, define when to use swaptions vs caps and floors.

Exercises for Chapter 12

1. Describe the basic "equilibrium" credit derivative pricing equation.

2. What are the similarities of credit derivative pricing models and binomial models? What are the differences?

3. Do credit derivative premiums have to track corporate bond spreads? If they don't track, what trade might you do?

4. When might the one year credit derivative premium be higher than the two year?

5. How would you mark credit derivatives to market?

6. How might you use credit derivatives to approximate a corporate bond?

7. Options exist on credit derivatives. How would you think about pricing them?

8. How would you price the "restructuring" default clause unique to credit derivatives?

Exercises for Chapter 13

1. It is stated that option pricing programs can price all the Greeks.
How would you measure Rho using an option pricing program?

2. What is the point of knowing the Greeks?

3. How are linear regression and beta and equity hedge ratios related?

4. If you know R Beta, what else do you need to get a hedge ratio?

4. Private equity investments are difficult to mark, they don't trade.
For this reason, we stressed "realized" flows only go into an IRR.
However, discuss how you would mark a private equity fund like a mutual fund.

5. In words, define the basic currency approach to value currency forwards.
If the forward trades differently than fair, what could be responsible?

6. What is the logic of the equation [sale price = NOI / cap rate]?
Is cap rate like any return you know?

7. Imagine you are going to build a strip mall. Create a business plan and define the potential return to an investor.

Exercises for Chapter 14

1. With a pool of assets, should one assume a term to legal final or
   weighted average maturity?

2. How does WAM differ from WAL?
   How does WAL differ from Duration?

3. Consider two pools with the same WAL.
   How could they differ in cash flows?

4. What do servicers get paid to do?

5. How are scheduled principal payments related to loan balance?
   Why aren't they constant over time?

6. Appendix 14C shows there is an smm used in defining scheduled and
   another for unscheduled.
   Why the difference - what drives each one?

7. The principal shrinkage of a tranche can be defined by a put spread
   as shown in Appendix 14C.
   How might you use that fact to measure volatility of pool principal payments?

Exercises for Chapter 15

1. What is the difference between the efficient frontier approach and Monte Carlo?

2. Why isn't the risk of a weighted combination of assets simply the weighted sum of the individual risks?

3. What would you expect the shape of an efficient frontier be?

4. What composes a period return in a Monte Carlo analysis? Where do the random numbers fit in?

5. What does the Cholesky adjustment adjust for?

6. The end return obtained in the example appears similar to the financing rate (3%). Is that a chance occurrence?

7. What should the mean result of a Monte Carlo be in a "risk-neutral" world?

Exercises for Chapter 16

1 What are the essential problems Dodd-Frank legislation tries to solve?

2 What are their solutions?

3 What are the potential problems with these "solutions"?

4 What would you propose as the problems and solutions to them?

Exercises for Chapter 17

1 Describe the GAAP treatment of a derivative at purchase of the derivative.

2 Assuming GAAP, if the derivative is not in a hedging transaction, what happens next reporting period if the derivative changes in value?

3 Assuming GAAP, if the derivative is in a hedging transaction, what happens next reporting period if the derivative changes in value?

4 Describe the STAT treatment of a derivative at purchase of the derivative.

5 Describe the STAT treatment of an asset at purchase of the security.

6 Describe how Character, Timing and Holding Period affects taxes.

7 What is an NOL and how can you net it against a gain?

Exercises for Chapter 18

I. Examples of Interest rate opportunities

1 You are a corporate treasurer.

    a. What are your considerations as to what debt you will issue in the future? (5y, 10y, Fixed,etc.)

    b. How will you hedge the debt?

    c. Calculate a hedge ratio.

    d. Calculate the "cost" of the hedge.

    e. Why is cost in quotes above?

2 Most derivatives can be assigned. What is that? Why is it valuable?

3 You are a mortgage banker.

    a. What is the problem a mortgage banker faces?

    b. How is that different from a corporate treasurer?

    c. What is the general nature of the best hedge?

    d. As a regulator, what would you do if you saw a mortgage banker only selling calls?

Exercises for Chapter 18, Cont'd

4 You work in a commercial bank. Imagine the basic business
is get money by issuing CD's and make money by lending.

    a. Under what circumstances would you hedge CD issuance?

    b. If you did, how would you do it and describe risks.

    c. Would you control lending by hedging also?

II. Examples of Credit opportunities.

1 What are the similarities and differences of buying a corporate
bond and selling protection using a credit derivative?

2 Same question but add a bond to the credit derivative.
Similarities and differences to a "regular" corporate bond.

II Examples of Equity opportunities.

1 How are employee stock options different
from regular stock options?

2 What differences would that cause in a Monte Carlo of the two?

3 You are an activist private equity manager.

    a. How will you get funds - what vehicle?

    b. How will you use those funds and be "active"?

    c. What is a proxy vote and how does it affect your activism?

Exercises for Chapter 18, Cont'd

IV Examples of Commodity opportunities.

    1 What commodity markets might be most easily manipulated?

    2 As a regulator, how would you discourage it?

V. Examples of Currency opportunities.

    1 What would you do if you wanted to "drive" a currency?

    2 As a regulator, how would you discourage it?

VI Examples of Real Estate opportunities.

    1 Assume your source of funds is private individuals.
    How would your investments differ in real
    estate as compared to a mutual fund source?
    Would there be differences in what you buy -
    whole loans vs securities, how levered you are, etc.

    2 What do you imagine the differences are between REITS,
    mutual funds, hedge funds investing in real estate?

    3 What did AIG do in sub prime mortgages. Why did they
    choose to invest in credit derivatives?

Exercises for Chapter 19

1 Create a business plan to set up a derivative trading program in

    a. An Investment bank

    b. A Commercial bank

    c. An Insurance company

    d. A Mutual fund

    e. A start-up retail organization (like a Schwab).

    f. A Hedge fund

    g. A Private Equity fund.

2 **How would a broader alternatives selection program be set up in the above entities?** That is, in #1 there is active trading. Here one is screening managers managing different alternatives.